LIFE AFTER

DEATH

An Interpretive Tool to Understanding Different Lived Expressions in Today's World

KENNETH LUKONG

TABLE OF CONTENT

ABBREVIATIONS

Wis	Wisdom
CCC	Catechism of the Catholic Church
Prov	Proverbs
Dan	Daniel
EN	Evangelii Nuntiandi

INTRODUCTION

In Luke 16:19-31, the rich man, after grinding his teeth in hell, solicits Abraham to send someone from the dead to caution his brothers who lived unrighteous lives, but Abraham does not grant the request. He says if they do not listen to the prophets, they will not listen to someone from the dead. Death is a fundamental and self-evident reality that, whether we accept it or not, we still experience at the end without any way to share our experiences with others. Since death is a given, Robert Jordan succinctly affirms that the importance of death does not lie in dying because we must die one day, but in how we face it because it is not the end of life. Death is a change to another form of existence, an idea which many consider a travesty. The concept of life after death is as old as humanity itself but it still escapes humanity's understanding for the most part, and humanity's acceptance of its existence. Given these mixed feelings about life after death, humans tend to live their lives according to how they understand the concept of life after death. To understand this concept profoundly, it is incumbent on us to look at how our understanding of death, consciously or unconsciously, shapes our living in this world.

Human existence is contingent and not wholly directed to its teleology because belief systems move teleology. For instance, my understanding of life after death largely determines how I live my life in this world. Advancements in

2

science and technology have shifted belief systems about the end of life. Scientific knowledge and advancements continually see death as the irreversible cessation of biological functions simply because there is no scientific proof of life after death.[1] This trend continually alienates man from the right belief that there is life here and life hereafter. Teleologically, man is created for God; as Augustine beautifully writes, "you have made us for yourself and our hearts are restless until they rest in you."[2] Man should live on this earth in the true likeness of God and should return to God, his creator, when his earthly life is ended. The means to this end is living a life worthy of our natural and Christian calling in order to be with God after death. However, because life and life after death are not wholly understood and lived in perspective, man's conception and understanding of life and life after death largely shapes how he lives his life in this world.

An understanding of life after death, therefore, becomes a hermeneutical tool to unlock myriad expressions of living in this world. Given the universality of death and the frequently unacceptable views about life beyond earthly life, it is necessary to study how various understandings of life after death are expressed in contemporary life. What is the dominant belief system about life after death, and how does this pull many to live in that particular way? Who are the remnants of Christianity and how do they survive in a pluralistic, secularized, and eschatologically deaf and numb society that continually diminishes a teleology of life because of scientific pursuits? How can one in such a situation still live

---

[1] "Death" in *The New Encyclopedia Britannica,* 15th ed. "death"

[2] Augustine, *The Confessions,* trans. Edward Bouverie Pusey (The Floating Press, 2008), 5.

3

in the manner of heaven despite prevailing theories about the nonexistence of life after death and the cessation of biological functions as the end of life? These questions, materialistic trivializations of death, and many more shall direct our research into a proper understanding of life after death as lived out in the contemporary world, and then a Christian understanding of life after death in the proceeding chapters.

This research is urgent because the harm that the contemporary dominant narratives continue to cause to authentic living with *telos* in mind can no longer be avoided. Slogans like "life is short so make the best out of it" have nihilistic undertones and continue to push man out of the direction of a life wholly lived for God. It is therefore urgent to unlock the various expressions of contemporary living in order to offer solutions, or at best bring to consciousness, the way these theories of life after death push us further from our goal and create confusion in our lives.

The urgency and import of this work can be seen from the universality and uncertainty about death. Death comes to us all, but we never know the time. It is therefore important to bring about a corrective to the various understandings of life after death that do not enhance a theology of hope in eschatological existence. Also, pointing out the various forms of life after death is important. For instance, there is heaven, hell, and purgatory, so that as much as the dominant narrative pulls us away, we are aware of future irreversible possibilities present in scriptures, tradition, and magisterial teachings about eschatological dimensions of life after life.

This work will be divided into three chapters. In chapter one, I will examine the various understandings of life after death. In this respect, I will look at views and ways of life that

4

are prominent and see how those beliefs continue to present a challenge to living eschatologically. In chapter two, I will examine the Church's understanding of eschatology as a corrective to the prevalent theories denying the world of the teleologically eschatological reality incumbent in every human life. Chapter three will attempt a hermeneutical corrective as an interpretive tool to all these expressions and demonstrate the need to pastorally engage contemporary man – in living eschatologically amid secularization and technological advancements that try to dethrone the Supreme Being from the eschatological reality that only God holds.

CHAPTER ONE

PROMINENT THEORIES OF LIFE AFTER DEATH

The understanding of life after death differs from person to person, culture to culture, and religion to religion. Prominent theories of life after death offer people a chance to reach an informed decision about what they understand before accepting a particular belief system. However, society is often moved by trending belief systems, which usually have a large impact on a particular group or generation. For instance, in today's world, atheistic scientism sees death as merely the cessation of biological functions, and so recognizes nothing like life after death. This understanding of death impresses millennials, but accomplishments in science and technology have had a negative impact on society at large. In this chapter, I shall examine some views on how people have understood life and life after death both past and present, but first we must know the state of the eschatological problem as it exists in today's world. Currents in contemporary understanding of death will help guide us as we consider prominent theories of life after death.

1.1. State of the Problem

It is not easy for many to understand death given that there is no personal experience from anyone on this subject. To that effect, a correct understanding of death continues to pose a problem to many in the world. Following are some of the prominent issues today that influence our understanding of death.

1.1.1. The Exact Sciences

We live in a technologically and scientifically advanced age wherein scientism claims to have answers to every question, and essential to this "scientism" is the fact that what science cannot account for simply does not exist or is unimportant. Science has made tremendous advances, but "issues of life and death are not among those which progress in the exact sciences can clarify," and thus "there is a set of questions--the really human questions--where other approaches towards an answer must be brought in."[3] Faced with this dilemma, a coalition of science and theology, faith and reason, should be key rather than a craving for separation or the non-existence of religion, because when faced with the "really human questions," like the "last things," as Ratzinger calls them, "the experience comprised in the wisdom of the tradition remains of central importance"[4] and should be sought to help answer the "really human questions." This entails seeking beyond science rather than being content with the

---

[3] Joseph Ratzinger, *Eschatology*: *Death and Eternal Life* (Washington D.C: The Catholic University of America Press, 1988), 72.

[4] Ratzinger, *Eschatology*: *Death and Eternal life*, 72.

extent the exact to which sciences can go. Thus, the credulous age, with its overt dogmatism in the exact sciences, does not help in this endeavor, so until man realizes the limits of science and the place of revelation on the question of death in particular and the "really human questions" in general, authentic solutions will always be missing thereby causing misunderstandings, even in Scriptures.

1.1.2. Misunderstandings of the Scriptures

The Bible is the soul of theology and was written under the inspiration of the Holy Spirit.[5] Despite this, the state of the eschatological question is continually misrepresented, and the misuse of Scriptures is rampant, as death "has undergone such a radicalization that its biblical aspect is visibly stripped away."[6] Some of the misunderstandings include modern exegesis and eisegesis, and the Bible itself being considered archaic. Ratzinger further affirms that many argue that the Bible has nothing to say about the resurrection or immortality. Historically, philosophers and others have struggled to seek an ideal in the liberation of matter. Plotinus seemed to "be embarrassed by the fact of having a body" and thus continually desired the liberation of matter.[7] This goes against Scripture's concern with the resurrection of the body. Sadly still, many read Psalms 38:6 to mean that since the lives punished by God end, there is no need to try living a Christian life.[8] Many do not know what is written in the Scriptures and

---

[5] Paul VI, *Dei Verbum* (Vatican: Vatican Press, 1965) n. 24.

[6] Joseph Ratzinger, *Eschatology: Death and Eternal life*, 74.

[7] Porphyry, *De Plotini vita 1: Plotin Schriften*, ed. R Harder, vol. 5, (Hamburg 1958), 2.

[8] Christopher Tuckett, *2 Thessalonians and Pauline Eschatology* (Leuven, Belgium: Petters, 2013), 205.

do not wish to know, thereby complicating the problem. Contemporary man, under the influence of scientism, largely sees the Bible as a mythos of the past, far removed from reality and that which invites man to vegetate in his primitive stupidity. In such misunderstanding and misrepresentation of scripture man is not seen "in his undivided wholeness and unity as God's creature and cannot be sliced down the middle into body and soul."[9] Therefore, it is only through a biblically sound understanding of death as presented in Scriptures, especially the resurrection narratives, that a correct finality of death will be reconstructed and embraced.

1.1.3. Fear of Death

Fear of the unknown has contributed to mankind's search for easy answers to the question of death. Given the lack of experience of what happens in death, many want to have ready-made answers, as if death were one of the experiential sciences. Fear of death causes many to reject a theology of death and life after death as unsound and unconvincing since rational-experiential evidence is lacking thereby adding to their anxiety. Ratzinger contends that the contemporary world even hides the reality of death as "even funeral homes themselves devise special arrangements so as to avoid mentioning the fact of death."[10] This kind of fear, then, never brings man to the stark reality of death in order to prepare adequately for it. Man must therefore get rid of all fear which does not, by any means, cancel the fear of dying, but rather makes man face it in a Christian manner as the new life and not a separation of matter from spirit.

---

[9] Ratzinger, *Eschatology: Death and Eternal life*, 74.

[10] Ratzinger, *Eschatology: Death and Eternal life*, 69.

1.1.4. Dualistic Conception of Man

The separation of man into matter and spirit or soul continually causes problems for the correct understanding of death. In biblical thought, man is seen as one and united as God's creature and cannot be talked of as body being distinct from the soul.[11] There is a difference between duality and dualism. Dualism implies "an anthropology in which the body is extrinsic to the soul. *The hypostatic union is the doctrine that says man has both human and divine attributes.* The situation of a union of body and soul is considered depressive, while the ideal is placed in the liberation of the soul with respect to the body."[12] On the other hand, duality strongly underlines man's unity and the separation of body and soul is "ontologically deficient with respect to their union."[13] This confusion of terms brings misunderstanding to the duality of man because of "the continuity and identity between the person who lived and the person who will rise, inasmuch as in virtue of such a survival the concrete individual never totally ceases to exist."[14] Duality affirms this continuity to the human person because at death, a conscious element survives. This survival continues until the moment of the Parousia because of the moment the psyche is separated with no reunion, we are in the realm of angels.[15]

---

[11] Ratzinger, *Eschatology: Death and Eternal Life*, 74.

[12] Franz Cumont, *Lux Perpetua*, (Paris, 1949), 390.

[13] Fischer R. Kathleen, *El pensamiento de Etienne Gilson* (Pamplona 1980), 224.

[14] Peter C. Phan, "Current Theology Contemporary Context and Issues in Eschatology," *Theological Studies* 55 (1994), 507-536.

[15] Orbe Antonio, *Antropologia de San Ireneo* (Madrid: 1969), 443.

Another difficulty in understanding the concept of duality as opposed to dualism is the theory of *thnetopsychism.* The theory asserts that the whole person dies, body and soul, and that if there is a resurrection, it is a new creation of the one who died *ex nihilo*. This sees in man a dualism that everything exists in pieces without continuity.[16]

I am man because I am a unity of body and soul and not body as distinct from soul because the two make one person. Scholars have examined why Paul used that image of the Church as the Body of Christ, and it is clear that

> *Paul had received the image of the body from the Hellenistic milieu, which got it specifically from an Aesop's fable wherein the various organs of the human body, out of jealousy, conspired against the stomach and no longer supplied it with food: all of them perished.*[17]

This sensual image explicates analogically how the human body functions and how distinct elements function as a unity of body and soul. Any attempt at separating body and soul, treating one with disgust, only ends in an inauthentic understanding of man and is at worst heretical.

---

[16] International Theological Commission, *Questions in Eschatology*, 221-225. This position of *thnetopsychism* was seen among the Tatians and some Arabian heretics. However, in rejection of this view and the fact that man should lean more to the language of duality and not dualism, *Questions in Eschatology* makes use of the Bible, especially Wisdom 16:13-14 and Matthew 10:28. Both texts affirm the power of God who can destroy both body and soul. He is the only one to be feared and not mortals. Mortals can destroy the body but cannot destroy the soul.

[17] Benoît-Dominique de la Soujeole, *Introduction to the Mystery of the Church* (Washington D.C: The Catholic University of America Press, 2014), 69.

11

This attempt to consider man in dualistic terms existed since the time of Plato. Matter or the body was looked upon as bad and only the spirit or soul considered positive, "God-like, the really real,"[18] in which only the wise understood and so treated "the body as the tomb of the soul [preparing it] for immortality through such enmity to the prison house." On such wisdom and understanding Plato's Socrates, a supporter of the idealist understanding of death, "celebrates his own dying as a festal journey from the sickness of bodily life to the health of true living" and pleaded for a sacrifice of thanksgiving to the gods when this separation finally happens.[19] Such is the lot of many today who do not understand that man is one unique being and that death is not a happy separation from the limitations of the body, but the beginning of new life, a transfigured body, as the resurrection of Christ signifies. Secularization, therefore, robs man of religious understanding.

1.1.5. Secularization

The International Theological Commission, in addressing perplexities in current eschatology, says that the contemporary world continues to be an enemy to Christian hope in the afterlife. Steve Bruce categorically states that secularism

> is a slow process of generational change in which people gradually lose interest in things that mattered to their parents and in which the possibilities for belief and practice expand while the salience of any of those beliefs and practices declines...The best way I can convey the change from religious to the

---

[18] Ratzinger, *Eschatology: Death and Eternal Life*, 73.

[19] Ratzinger, *Eschatology: Death and Eternal Life*, 73.

12

secular is to use the metaphor of an abandoned garden in the countryside. Without constant pruning, selective breeding, and weeding, the garden loses its distinctive character, as it is overtaken by the greater variety of plant species in the surrounding wilderness.[20]

The world's affinity to secularism, which "consists in an autonomous vision of humanity and of the world, a vision that prescinds from the dimension of mystery, neglecting or even denying this dimension,"[21] cannot be overlooked. Such immanentism, Bruce continues, "is a diminution of the total picture of man."[22] The negation of the mystery that man is created to live in and die for brings about the contemporary loss of a sense of the sacred and hope in a life after life. These secularistic tendencies seek "by every means to cast into oblivion death and those questions that are inevitably linked with it…[and] hope is shattered by a pessimism regarding the goodness of human nature itself, a pessimism arising from the increase in distress and affliction."[23] Unfortunately, this pessimism did not subside after the cruelty of the Second World War, but the advance of secularism caused industrious nations to lend to the contemporary idolatry of consumerism rather than being optimistic about human nature and

---

[20] *Steve Bruce, Secularization: In Defense of an Unfashionable Theory* (NY: Oxford University Press, 2011), 19.

[21] International Theological Commission, *Some Currents Questions in Eschatology*, vol. II, Texts and Documents 1986-2007 (1992), 56.

[22] Synod Fathers, *Relatio Finalis*, II, A, 1 (E Civitate Vaticana, 1985), 6.

[23] International Theological Commission, *Some Currents Questions in Eschatology*, vol. II, Texts and Documents 1986-2007, (1992), 57-58.

eschatological hope, which will be void of human demeaning and destruction.[24] Secularism continues to increase the doubt whether death leads to annihilation or to new life. European countries, largely and surprisingly enough, consciously or unconsciously have adapted the attitude of annihilation which is the fruit of secularism, and this is purposefully seen in religious indifferentism hovering over the world like a roaring lion devouring souls.

Religious indifferentism brings to the fore doubts about hope in life, whether it "consists in the promise of God given through Jesus Christ or is to be based on some other savior to be hoped for."[25] Such misunderstandings and misrepresentations have degenerated into the quagmire of material-secularistic trivializations we experience today.

1.2. Prominent Theories of Life after Death

1.2.1. Reincarnation

Reincarnation and its Greek equivalents *metempsychosis* or *metemsomatosis* "describe a doctrine which holds that the human soul assumes another body after death. It has, that is, a new incarnation or enfleshment."[26] Souls that have been found to be unclean or tarnished at death will need another life to be purified from every stain to enjoy eternal bliss. To this effect, the process of

---

[24] Synod Fathers 1985, *Relatio Finalis*, II, D, 1 (E Civitate Vaticana, 1985), 17.

[25] International Theological Commission, *Some Currents Questions in Eschatology*, vol. II, Texts and Documents 1986-2007, (1992), 55-94.

[26] L. Scheffczyk, Der Reinkarnationsgedanke in der altchristlichen Literatur (Manchen, 1985), 28.

metempsychosis is cyclical until the soul(s) in question have attained the perfection desired for seeing God face to face.[27]

Belief in reincarnation has continued to grow in such a manner that diverse forms persist in the world today. The Pew Research conducted in November 2021 shows that 33% of adult Americans believe in reincarnation.[28] This tells us that the growth rate is phenomenal and we need to watch out especially by teaching the authentic doctrine about life after death. Reincarnation is the belief that people "have already passed through an earlier life and will have another life on earth, or who at least hope that their soul will enjoy further life cycles (migration of the soul)."[29] In this light, life after death is seen as a return to the same life lived before. Some reasons for this belief include the presence of many earthly existences, so we have lived before and will live again. Also, believers in reincarnation claim there is a natural law that continues to impel all towards perfection. Because of the shortness of earthly existence, this perfection is not met, so there must be some way to continue this project. Moreover, adherents of reincarnation affirm that man's ultimate destination is the achievement of his hard work and so in "every new existence, the soul progresses in virtue of its own strivings." Any wrong done is retributed new and difficult reincarnations.[30]

---

[27] Vatican II, *Schema Constitutiones Dogaticae de Ecclesia*, n.7.

[28] Pew Research, accessed at: https://baptistnews.com/article/pew-study-offers-some-surprising-insights-to-american-views-on-suffering-salvation-heaven-and-hell/#.YlRQ6C1h23U on March 18th 2022.

[29] Hans Schwarz, *Eschatology* (William B. Eerdmans Publishing Company, Grand Rapids: Michigan, 2000), *302*.

[30] International Theological Commission, *Some Questions in Eschatology*, n.9.

Another view asserts that in death the "persisting self-conscious ego will continue to exist after bodily death" because very few people go straight to heaven. Those who go immediately to heaven, those "whom the religions call saints or buddhas or arhats or *jivanmuktas* have fulfilled the purpose of temporal existence, which is the gradual creation of perfected persons- their perfection consisting…in a self-transcending state beyond separate ego-existence."[31] Apart from these few, everyone who dies in a non-perfected state continues to exist somewhere "in time as distinct egos."[32] Eternity is timeless, so when John Hick considers our existence in time, it is clear that it is in this world, although he is not certain where precisely. The belief in reincarnation is the means to become perfected for final eschatological completion.

For example, Lucky Dube,[33] a South African singer, in his song "Big Boys Don't Cry" talks about reincarnation as a chance to complete that which people could not do in their present lives. He laments the attitude of himself and his purported lover who felt drawn towards each other, but no one said anything. Finally, they ran short of time to enter into a love affair. Lucky Dube then says if they both believe in reincarnation, they will both have the chance to love each other. The idea of reincarnation continues to grow and reincarnationists see death as the possibility in progressive

---

[31] John Hick, *Death and Eternal Life* (New York: Harper, 1976), 399.

[32] Hick, *Death and Eternal Life*. 399.

[33] This song was released on the 2nd of November 1987. Given the trend of things and the popularity of Lucky Dube, it gained wide acceptance and understanding as many believed in the reincarnation.

evolution.   But where does this idea originate in the public imagination?

In the *Origin of Species*, Charles Darwin, as interpreted by Schwarz, focuses on the present and on the future when talking about progress and perfection. He asserts that "as natural selection works solely by and for the good of each being, all corporeal and mental endowments will tend to progress towards perfection."[34] Putting things in perspective, Darwin concludes, "From the war of nature, from famine and death, the most exalted object which we are capable of conceiving namely, the production of the higher animals, directly follows."[35] Because he affirms that the most exalted object we can think of as "the production of the higher animal," it is clear that this is the belief in a perfection that only happens in this world. If Darwin was interested in life beyond this world, he would not refer to a higher animal, but rather to spirits or angels.

Frederick Nietzsche wrote in 1883 about the "Superman" who is "higher than humanity" in *Thus Spake Zarathustra*. Nature conceived of a Superman as "the meaning of the earth." He worked for the fact that humanity should be overcome because "the Superman is far above humanity as humanity is above the apes."[36] The Superman will be rare to find just as great things are for the great, but that the Superman, "will be the next stage in human

---

[34] Charles Darwin, *The Origin of Species by Means of Natural Selection or the Preservation of Favoured Races in the Struggle for Life* (Chicago, 1952), 243.

[35] Charles Darwin, *The Origin of Species*, 243.

[36] Freidrich Nietzsche, *Thus Spake Zarathustra* LXXIII/2, in *The Complete Work,* ed. Oscar Levy, (New York: Macmillan, 1924), 11:351.

evolution."[37] This achievement is not the life after death but will come about through some form of evolution. Evolution becomes the perfection of humanity that has decided to revalue itself, so the idea of life after death is out of the question. In fact, there is nothing like life after death because for Nietzsche God is dead, and everything ends in nothingness.

1.2.2. Scientific Materialism

Scientific materialism seeks to convince its adherents that the "ironclad laws of nature do not allow for heavenly interruption, whether by divine miracles or by a divinely decreed end of the world."[38] To this end, this system refers to the law of energy conservation to make its point; namely, that within an isolated energy system, the amount of energy used always remains the same. Any energy that leaves reenters the world in a different form. The materialists then conclude that the universe will always be the same, with no beginning or an end, and most importantly, its future will be a modification in its past.[39] Humanity and the universe are viewed from a naturalistic perspective, while the spiritual processes are mere physiological causes. Paul Heinrich Dietrich von Holback, therefore, describes man as a "product of nature which is subjected to the laws of the physical

---

[37] Samuel Enoch Stumpf and James Fieser, *Philosophy: History and Problems,* 7th ed. (Boston: MA: McGraw Hill, 2008), 367.

[38] Schwarz, *Eschatology*, 176.

[39] Frederick Copleston, *A History of Philosophy (New York:* Double Day 1975), 78-79.

universe. Beyond that there are no further ultimate principles or powers."[40]

According to Schwarz's understanding of Ludwig Feuerbach, the survival instinct in humans is evidence that no one wants to die. It is only in the realm of Christianity that this negative desire is made to look positive, that there is an afterlife. He further claims that reason cannot explain how this happens, and that the resurrection of Christ occurred to satisfy man's desire for his immediate quests, which cannot be satisfied.[41] He further wonders why Christianity makes immortality the most certain part of its belief system because he sees it as the most uncertain. He, therefore, dismisses the idea of the resurrected person in heaven because he sees in the resurrection the denial of matter; even after death, there must be food and drink as there is no "disembodied existence possible."[42]

Primitive materialism goes a step further than current scientific materialism. It affirms the resurrection of the dead but speaks also of reanimation. In this respect, primitive materialism intimates that "we would reassume in resurrection the same matter, the same flesh and the same bones as in this life."[43] To an extent, it might be considered as reincarnation, but it is not. In the form in which we see

---

[40] Shwarz, *Eschatology*, 175.

[41] Hans Schwarz's understaning of Feuerback in his book Eschatology. Feuerbach Ludwig, *The Essence of Christianity* (New York: Harper Torchbooks, 1957), 135.

[42] Feuerback Ludwign, *Die Unsterblichkeitsfrage vom Standpunkt der Anthropologie*, 10:231.

[43] Mark Jordan, ed., *The Church's Confession of Faith: A Catholic Catechism for Adults*, trans. Stephen Arndt, (San Francisco: Ignatius Press, 1987), 338.

materialism today, it largely avoids talking about the resurrection as gaining transformed bodies but argues that it is impossible to lose that which belongs to one because everything that goes comes back through another avenue.

Feuerbach and the materialists conclude that because there is improvement in the world, it is unsound to talk about a religious or a theological future. There can be no reasoning faculties without matter, they say, and so by setting a goal of the beyond, Christianity has weakened the human potential to reach a better life and thereby cheats humanity of its utmost potential. The materialists, therefore, see no sense in eschatology because the world revolves, its energy is never wasted, and any thought or talk of the supernatural and life hereafter only limits our existential potential.

1.2.3. Secular Existentialism

According to Søren Kierkegaard, life is a journey whose sustenance was the graciousness of God.[44] However, secular existentialism has robbed us of this gracious God, saying that fundamental questions evade the grasp of man, whose existence has nothing to do with eschatology but just a "being-there" and "being-in-the-world," and "being-unto-death," the *Da-sein*. Temporality and death are irreplaceable factors of the Dasein because we all must face death. The anxiety caused by this existential reality should be seen as constitutive of who we are, rather than to try to evade anxiety by talking about life after death. Heidegger sees doing so as living inauthentically because anxiety is basic to our "being-there" and "being-in-the-world." As a "being-towards-death,"

---

[44] Martin Heidegger, *Being and Time*, trans. J. Macquarrie and E. Robinson (London: SCM, 1962), 234.

any explanation or philosophizing to say there is a life after life only blurs the *Dasein's ownmost* potentiality-for-Being.[45] In this light, there should be no talk about life after death because existence occurs only in this world and, there are not two worlds.

In the same light, for Jean-Paul Sartre, humanity is seen as "basically free of its destiny."[46] The way we look at the world and human relations and how we shape them is a result of our total freedom. In fact, humanity is "condemned to be free."[47] In this freedom, we have neither God, nor values, nor truth, and any talk about them only curtails our freedom. He further claims that our existence precedes our essence since our essence is simply our past. However, there are no common essences because we make our essences as we live our lives. Basically, we have to be-for-ourselves because there is nothing hereafter; unless we live for ourselves, we cannot avoid "bad faith." "Bad faith" or *mauavise foi* is Sartre's term which is simply a reliance on the past and a projection to the future because we just have to venture to the future without relying on either past or projection into the future.[48] Sartre totally rejects any possibility or talk about a future life because everything should concern the here and now. Life only has meaning if we live it piecemeal without any projection

---

[45] Martin Heidegger, *Being and Time*, trans. J. Macquarrie and E. Robinson (London: SCM, 1962), 234.

[46] Hans Schwarz, *The Human Being, A Theological Anthropology* (MA: William B. Eerdmans Publishing Company, Grand Rapids, 2013), 88.

[47] Sartre, *Being and Nothingness: An Essay on Phenomenological Ontology* (New York: Philosophical Library Press, 1956), 485.

[48] Sartre, *Being and Nothingness*, 70.

or regrets of our past. Therefore, eschatological discussions are irrelevant.

The secular existentialists view life as simply being-there, being-in-the-world, or being-for-itself and do not value any reliance on the past or the future because past and future cannot give reliant guidance for life. Life should be about the now as to be presented below because there is no life after death, as God has been killed according to Nietzsche.

1.2.4. The Death of God

Nietzsche proclaimed the death of God in *The Gay Science* in 1882. Many people have come to believe in this philosophy and lead lecherous and immoral lives because there is nothing to hope for after this life is ended. Nietzsche says God is dead and it is we who have killed him, and in so doing we have become gods; because all gods are dead, only the Superman lives now.[49] Proponents of this philosophy say there is no reward or punishment for any kind of life we live here on earth, and we can live as we want because God is dead. The death of God expresses itself in an existence that has no bearing on the life after death. Life ends in nothingness.

Central to the nihilist's position which Nietzsche is an advocate, is the fact that life ends in death. With the technical age's definition of death as the cessation of functions, death becomes the end of human life, which makes sense for them because God is dead. Nothing happens after one dies since

---

[49] Jürgen Moltmann, *Theology of Hope* (San Francisco: Harper, 1965), 170.

"there is no disembodied existence possible."[50] It becomes clear from the preceding that the nihilistic approach to death is a material trivialization because life actually transcends physical death since in the resurrection of the death, our bodies are transformed as was Christ's.

1.2.5. Marxist Optimism

Karl Marx and neo-Marxists are devoted to one goal, namely, to bring about a new world through revolution.[51] They are confident in a world without God, which inevitably ends here. Marx's endeavor is therefore to show that there is no life after, as there is no God. To this end he states, "the Philosophers have only interpreted the world, in various ways: the point, however, is to change it."[52] Karl Marx was inspired to change the world from the progressive industrialization and popularized Darwinism at his time. He strongly felt that the self-alienation of man in the name of religion is not sufficient since religion is also a "social product" that belongs to modern capitalism. His contemporary and colleague Frederick Engels claims that Christianity and socialism have much in common. For instance, "both Christianity and the workers' socialism preached forthcoming salvation from bondage and misery; Christianity places the salvation in a life beyond, after death, in heaven; socialism places it in this world, in a transformation of society...Three hundred years after its appearance Christianity was the recognized state religion in the Roman

---

[50] Ludwig Feuerbach, *Die Unsterbllichkeitsfrage vom Standpunkt der Anthropologie*, 10:236.

[51] Karl Marx, *Thesis on Feuerbach* (New York: Schocken Books, 1964) 72.

[52] Karl Marx, *Thesis on Feuerbach* (New York: Schocken Books, 1964) 72.

World Empire, and in barely sixty years socialism has won itself a position which makes its victory absolutely certain."[53]

In my understanding of Karl Marx, socialism's significance is obvious, thereby derailing humanity from preparing for the eschaton because Christianity did not seem to accomplish the needed social transformation in this world, but taught that it can only be achieved beyond, in the impending millennium. Christianity simply preaches cowardice, self-contempt, abasement, submission, and dejection, which are the direct opposite of the values of the proletariats.[54]

With the continual inculcation of these religious values, the longing for a better beyond and not a better earth thereby makes religion the "sign of the oppressed creature."[55] Karl Marx and his followers believe that there is no beyond, so this life must be lived to the fullest. Life ends on earth. Everything that one can do to live a better life cannot be abhorred because religion simply teaches one to be content with one's present misery and like the "Trials of Brother Jero,"[56] we eventually die without ever having our wishes and desires materialized. Therefore, there is no need to hope for a better eschatological tomorrow proposed by religion since it is the

---

[53] Friedrich Engels, On the History of Early Christianity, 316.

[54] Karl Marx, *The Communism of the Paper Rheinischer Beobachter*, 84.

[55] Karl Marx, *Contribution to the Critique of Hegel's Philosophy of Right*, 41.

[56] This is a play written by Wole Soyinka, a Nigerian writer who beautifully captures the struggle of quack prophets in the "business" of religion. They continually deceive their followers until they go to their graves without ever having their dreams fulfilled (Wole Soyinka, *The Trials of Brother Jero*, Dramatists Play Service, Inc., 1998, 11-20).

"opium of the masses" but for better society to live in the present with joy, making use of any means to achieve this end.

1.2.6. The Eschatological Skeptics

Skepticism is a philosophical school of thought that doubts everything, putting everything in the light of intellectual reason, and by so doing claims there are no universal truths. Skeptics teach that everything needs to be subjected to doubt because man is not sure of anything with certainty. The word originates from Greek *skeptikoi* and to the Greeks it meant *seekers* or *inquirers.* They doubted that Aristotle had discovered the truth about the world.[57] In theology, this term adopts the qualifier "eschatological" skepticism, which means doubters of eschatology. Proponents of this philosophy propound that even if we were to affirm that eschatology is the truth or that there is life after death, no one can prove it. No one has ever gone to heaven nor come back to life after dying, so it is impossible to talk about and believe that which cannot be experienced.

At the dawn of modern philosophy, René Descartes equally subjected everything to doubt and said that in everything, methodic doubt should be employed until proven otherwise.[58] Eschatological skeptics therefore subject everything about the afterlife and its doctrines to doubt if they are one day proven wrong, then they will believe. Thus, they

---

[57] Samuel Enoch Stumpf and James Fieser, *Philosoph: History and Problems*, 103.

[58] Rene Descartes, *Discourse on the Method and Meditation on First Philosopshy* (Indiapolis, Hackett Publishing Company 1949), 4.

live without any future in mind and enjoy the present because life ends at death.

Closely related to the notion of skepticism is atheism. Atheism is the belief in the non-existence of God. Unlike the eschatological skeptic, an atheist is certain and believes that God does not exist. He or she knows of only one life, here on earth, and so does not live according to any belief of an afterlife. Atheists live in the present because they do not only doubt life after death, but they are sure it does not exist. They attribute everything to chance, so whatever happens to them is just a process of chance.

1.2.7. Origenism

Origenism holds that souls come into this world because they are undergoing punishment for sins they committed in their first spiritual existence, so they need purification for those sins.[59] This world is therefore seen as a ground to make amends for sins committed in the previous life. This theory does not account for where and when that life took place. It further affirms that if, at the end of a person's time here on earth he or she is still not in right relation with God and in a state of grace to merit heaven, then their purification continues in hell till the person is fully converted. By this stand, the Origenists teach that there is conversion in hell. Hell is then looked upon as a state of purification, a place where one is converted if that process did not finish during the pilgrim life on earth.[60] This however goes against the Church's doctrine that teaches that the rightful place for purification is

---

[59] *Historical Errors Concerning the Vision of God*, Ch. 5. And Errors Concerning Hell, ch.5.

[60] Jean Danielou, *Son Univers [de Origenes] est un monde de libertes, Origene*, (Paris, 1948), 207.

purgatory and not hell. By this assertion, the Origenists do not know if this is their first time coming to earth, or whether they had another existence prior to this one.

Once the purification is complete, souls experience *apokatastasis.* This is the doctrine that explains that once souls are purified, then everything is restored to God in a state of blessedness. It goes further to affirm that because humans have the liberty to do whatever they will, there will always be subsequent sins after every purification, so the process continually repeats itself. This is because there is no possibility to arrive at new decisions even in the state of vision which is posterior to *apokatastasis.* The beginning of another new cycle of purification is the result of sin. In this process, therefore, there is no end to life on this earth because there will never be a time that souls are in an everlasting state of grace. Life then will continue in this process timelessly.[61] There is no account of where the souls originated or for how long they will continue in this process. This puts human life in a situation that is hard to comprehend as there is no linear progression to God.

1.2.8. Futuristic Eschatology

For Jürgen Moltmann and Wolfhart Pannenberg, Christianity is an eschatological faith. They are largely convinced that eschatology is more concerned with the future than it is about the present, although they include elements of presentism in their works. Moltmann speaks of a theology of hope grounded in the coming of God's kingdom, while Pannenberg writes of a future fulfilment of God's kingdom

---

[61] Candido Pozo, *Theology of the Beyond*, trans Mark A. Pilon, (St Paul's, New York 2018), 416.

which can be anticipated in our lives. Pannenberg says that in the beginning was the end, or the end is the beginning, thereby focusing on the end of the world. However, he neglects to respond to the idea that in the very beginning, God set the future of the world.[62]

Moltmann is preoccupied with the problem of the future because he establishes the whole of his theology around hope.[63] For him, therefore, the formula of Anselm *fides quarens intellectum* is replaced by *spes quaerens intellectum*, hope which seeks to understand or a learned hope (*docta fe*). In this way, Moltmann distances himself from the presentism of Rudolph Bultmann. Faith, he says, is the priority in the Christian life, but hope has primacy because everything is built on hope. It is in this light that he talks deeply about the importance of the resurrection of Christ for the Christian faith. He avers, "Christianity stands or falls with the reality of the raising of Jesus from the dead by God"; and, "A Christian faith that is not resurrected faith, can, therefore be called neither Christian nor faith."[64] Along these same lines, he concludes that the meaning of the resurrection and its interpretation is left to the future.[65] Moltmann therefore sees eschatology as a fully futuristic event with little or no bearing on the present. In this regard, he devotes his energy in the *Theology of Hope* to discussing the future, thereby missing out on the present life which prepares us for the future eschaton. In fact, we ought to live this pilgrim life eschatologically before we die. Just as

---

[62] Pannenberg Wolfgang, *Systematic Theology* (Michigan: Grand Rapids, Eerdmans Publishing, 1991), 166.

[63] Moltmann, *Theology of Hope*, 11.

[64] Moltmann, *Theology of Hope*, 150.

[65] Moltmann, *Theology of Hope*, 197.

the existential eschatologists or presentists missed on the future, futuristic eschatology misses on the importance of the presence in a progression that it is one life. The resurrection will be transformed bodies, not altogether new bodies.

1.2.9. Millennialism

Millennialism takes its roots from Revelation 20:1-15. It comes from the Latin "one thousand years" or *chiliasm*, whose meaning is the same in Greek.[66] Millennialism has a long development that involves Joachim of Fiore, postmillennialism, amillennialism, and dispensational premillennialism. This section will examine what these stand for in relation to eschatology.

Premillennialism "holds that Christ will return to the earth prior to the last day in order to exercise rule over the nations for a thousand years in the last stage of human history."[67] Millennialism, despite widespread favor and support, has never been a distinctive teaching of the Church. Today, variants like postmillennialism and others do exist, but the Church teaches that God will come in the Parousia and there is no indication of a thousand years of rule before the Parousia.

Postmillennialism, according to Schwarz, is more optimistic than millennialism. It expects a future prosperity prior to the coming of Christ. This idea was fueled by the emerging American nation with many hoping for better living as they await the coming of Christ since his return will inaugurate an eternal kingdom of bliss and peace. In the period before the coming of Christ, postmillennials expect that

---

[66] Hans Schwarz, Eschatology, 331

[67] Schwarz, *Eschatology*, 331.

the Church would have evangelized the world. Its greatest hope is in the proclamation of the Gospel and the conversion of hearts and minds according to the will of Christ.[68]

Amillennialism also does not consider any hope for a millennium but asserts that there will not be any future golden age for the Church in this world. Christ's rule will only be established in the spiritual sphere and not in the physical world.[69]

Dispensational premillennialism lays the foundation for premillennial ideologies. In this way, it asserts that "human history is divided into a series of ages (dispensations) in which humanity is tested with respect to some revealed aspect of God's will."[70] This division consist of seven stages. In each case or stage, human failure is judged by God and then we are taken to another step, which Hans Schwarz calls "new covenant conditions."[71] The seven divisions in dispensational premillennialism include "innocence (in the garden), conscience (up to the flood), human government (since Babel), promise (since Abraham), law (since Moses), grace (since Christ), and kingdom, the coming of the millennium."[72] The age of grace terminates when Christ comes unrecognized.[73] These stages are biblically structured from the time of innocence to the coming of Christ. Christ's coming brings grace for humanity but unfortunately according to the

---

[68] Schwarz, *Eschatology*, 332.

[69] Schwarz, *Eschatology*, 332.

[70] Schwarz, *Eschatology*, 332.

[71] Schwarz, *Eschatology*, 332.

[72] Schwarz, *Eschatology*, 322-333.

[73] Schwarz, *Eschatology*, 333.

dispensational premillennialist, the end of the age of grace is the unforeseen coming of Christ for his Church, the rapture, which affects both the "living and --- by partial resurrection--- the dead in Christ."[74]

Although this ideology is steeped in Scriptures, it does not teach exactly how the Christian waiting for an afterlife should be done. It has the idea of an afterlife, but the means to it is rapture after the seventh epoch of grace. Its elaborate futurology has a strong attraction for many. This is problematic because in this world, we should already live eschatologically since the kingdom of God is the "already" and "not yet.' In such fashion, it tries to ascribe modern world happenings to prophetic Scriptures. This is key to millennial eschatological thinkers. Unfortunately, it appropriates the world's mess as a blessing since to them Christ will repair the world. Worse still, dispensational premillennialism abrogates social responsibility other than one's duty as a citizen.[75] It is contrary to living wholly and eschatologically because one lives in society, and one's social responsibilities remain an integral part of my living as a Christian in the light of heaven. Dispensational premillennialism gives a false joy in the face of imminent calamity. It interprets unfortunate events and happenings as the rapture, the approaching of the end times, thereby giving false hope of the Parousia. In this way, divine election is absolutized and human freedom diminished.[76] This imbalance in man's freedom and divine election misconstrues the understanding of man as a being who fulfils his duties in a social context because of the freedom given to him by the

---

[74] Schwarz, *Eschatology*, 333.

[75] Schwarz, *Eschatology*, 333.

[76] Schwarz, *Eschatology*, 333.

absolute.[77] Thus, this ideology, as quoted by Schwarz, has pushed many to leave aside the freedom bestowed on them by God and enjoy the moment, rather than a glorification of calamitous acts as signs of the Parousia "since Christians will be spared the final tribulations [because] at the time of the rapture the saints meet Christ in the air, while at the second coming Christ returns to the mount of Olives to meet the saints on earth."[78] This gives the false hope that being a citizen of heaven is all that it entails without engaging in social responsibility. Sainthood, according to the dispensational premillennialists, is not achieved by words and deed, but merely by affirming oneself as a citizen of heaven. This false hope drummed into people produce deficiencies in living eschatologically in different parts of the world, and the most frequent deficiency is the doctrine of determinism / predeterminism.

1.2.10.   Determinism

The problem of determinism calls to question the disputable study of human freedom. If man is free, then how can man be determined since we are "free and autonomous beings who are responsible for the actions that we perform? "[79] For instance, some people believe that laws of nature govern everything. Others think there is an omnipotent God who is the cause of everything. Living eschatologically is and should be based upon the fact that we have moral freedom,

---

[77] Schwarz, *Eschatology*, 333.

[78] John F. Walvoord, *The Rapture Question* (Dunham: Grand Rapids, 1964), 8.

[79] Joseph Keim Campbell et al., *Freedom and Determinism* (MA: Cambridge, Bradford Book, 2004), 1.

which is a "necessary precondition for our being accountable for our actions."[80]

There are many kinds of determinism,[81] but for the purposes of the topic, theological determinism shall be the focal point. Theological determinism claims that an all-knowing God "determines the course of events by conserving the world in a law-like way, and He conserves the world and its contents by continuously creating them...[His] upholding created substance, or causing its existence in each successive moment, is altogether equivalent to an immediate production out of nothing."[82] This amounts to the fact that everything that happens is a total and exclusive causal activity wrought by God, even those that happen through natural causes, since God is the originator of all. Most importantly, it is not within the power of frail humanity to "cause God to will what He does, and no human person has the power to frustrate the efficacy of the divine will."[83]

Neal Judisch presents another version of theological determinism, which has affinities with medieval Aristotelian and early modern concurrentism. God, according to this version, is still the one who sustains the universe, remaining

---

[80] Joseph Keim Campbell et al., *Freedom and Determinism,* 1.

[81] Logical determinism states that all propositions including those dealing with the future actions must either be true or false. Temporal determinism "claims that time is another dimension like any of the other three spatial dimension, so that the difference between what is in your past and what is in your future is a lot like the difference between what is to your left and what is to your right." Also, causal determinism advocates those past facts with the natural law project the future facts. Campbell et al., *Freedom and Determinism,* 1.

[82] Neal Judisch, "Theological Determinism and the Problem of Evil," in *Religious Studies* 44 (2008) 167.

[83] Judisch, "Theological Determinism and the Problem of Evil," 168.

the direct and total cause of all that happens.[84] But we are not in control of our actions, and for anyone to be free with respect to an action is to have a certain level of control over that action.[85] Contemporary individuals who do not want to live eschatologically now are brainwashed by the fact that everything is already determined by God. This remains untrue because God as omniscience knows everything we are ever going to do, but what we do is a free, undetermined decision wrought by our free will.

1.2.11.   The Spiritual Heritage of Joachim de Fiore

This spiritual heritage of Joachim grew from the Middle Ages with Joachim of Fiore, whose intent was to create an "innerworldly eschatology." Joachim insists that our earthly history is within us and so salvation, which transcends this earthly kingdom, is of lesser interest. To this, he continued that the kingdom of God is in the third age, a society that has no divisions where the "eternal gospel" (Rev. 14:6-7) and the kingdom of the Spirit are to thrive; it comes in a unique and secularized form.[86] With this framework, an eschaton is brought within historical times which is not the "ultimate absolute, but as a relative absolute."[87] With this secularization, what is of eschatological import is passed over in silence and "one places oneself within the perspective of a

---

[84] Judisch, "Theological Determinism and the Problem of Evil," 170-171.

[85] Judisch, "Theological Determinism and the Problem of Evil," 170-171.

[86] Michael Sharkey and Thomas Weinandy eds., International Theological Commission in *Some Current Questions in Eschatology*, 1992, 58.

[87] Michael Sharkey and Thomas Weinandy eds., International Theological Commission in *Some Current Questions in Eschatology*, 1992, 58.

temporal messianism."[88] This tendency of Joachim of Fiore has influenced many who no longer accept real hope in the future. His historico-eschatological conceptions tend to confuse many. Today, Neo-Joachims have drifted even further from his history of the ages especially in contemporary times with the love of temporal messianisms and the relative absolute. These continue to trivialize eschatological conceptions of the kingdom.

In this chapter, I have examined various theories and conceptions with which people look at life after death as a means to understand contemporary living. In this light, we saw that the state of the problem encompasses a wide range of issues, among which was growth in the exact sciences, fear or phobia of death, and secularism. These and many others set the stage in understanding current issues in this field of eschatology. Among the ways contemporary humanity continues to understand life after death, reincarnation, scientific materialism, death of God, Marxist optimism, and so on demonstrate that those who believe in one or the other are misinformed about life after death. These ideologies and theories continually deprive mankind of the true eschatological realism so that man can live in preparation for the coming kingdom. These tendencies have become deeply rooted in the society and, like Joachim de Fiore and his followers, continue to convince people to abandon the true and authentic hope in life after death after our earthly pilgrimage is ended.

---

[88] Congregation of the Doctrine of the Faith, *Libertatis Nuntius*, (Instruction on Certain Aspects of the Theology of Liberation), 10, 6, AAS 76, 1984, 901.

Amid such conflicting and destructive theories about life after death, the solution is to undertake a coherent understanding of salient eschatological issues that can help our day to day living and pastorally help individuals struggling with such theories by presenting in sum tenets of what the Church understands and teaches about life after death.

if you are enjoying this book leave a review for the author on amazon Thank you!

CHAPTER TWO

THE CHURCH'S UNDERSTANDING AND TEACHING ABOUT LIFE AFTER DEATH

In the previous chapter, I examined prominent theories about death and life after death, showing that there are materialistic-secularizing-trivializing ideologies and theories continually at work concerning the question of eschatology in general. These theories incessantly gain merit and mature in a clamoring, secularized society where the credulity of the masses is largely seen as being in opposition to God. The increasing number of nominal Christians and non-Christians make a correct understanding of life after death cumbersome, especially with the prevailing theories above. The fundamental questions of life which should condition the way of life are: Who am I? Where am I from? Where am I going? How do I get there? He who has no 'wherefrom' will hardly have a 'whereto' and therefore will lack a concrete 'wherein'. The hope and belief in a life hereafter, directly connected and dependent on the life now, will answer these concerns.

In this light, therefore, it is important to delve into a correct understanding of life after death as a corrective to the prevailing doctrines that continually compromise vital aspects of a wholistic understanding of life after death. It is hoped that through this treatment, "no one ought to be ashamed of the natural feelings of repugnance which are experienced in the face of death, since our Lord himself willed to suffer these before his own death, and Paul testifies that he had experienced them: 'We do not wish to be stripped naked but to be clothed again' (2 Cor 5:4)."[89] This quote makes it clear that repugnance of death should not be avoided but embraced, since Christ died to save us.

In order to get a deeper treatment of the Church's understanding of life after death as a corrective to the prominent theories in Chapter 1, this chapter will examine the meaning and understanding of life after death, the biblical basis of eschatology, the resurrection of Christ as a fundament to our hope, eternal life and its elements in the New Testament, the purifying state of purgatory, the problem of hell and *Sheol*, and the Parousia.

2.1. The Meaning and Scope of Eschatology

The term "eschatology" is derived from the Greek word *eschaton*, which means "last." It therefore represents the idea in systematic theology "devoted to last or final things, such as death and judgment, heaven and hell, and the end of the world."[90] Therefore, the study of eschatology involves the

---

[89] International Theological Communion, in *Some Current Questions in Eschatology*, 77.

[90] Bill T. Arnold, "Old Testament Eschatology and the Rise of Apocalypticism in Historical Eschatology," in *The Oxford Handbook of*

study of the world, end times, and the resurrection of Christ as its basis.[91] However, the theology of eschatology emerged well before the term "eschatology" was commonly used.

The first known treatise on eschatology, *Prognosticon future saeculi,* was written by St. Julian of Toledo in the 7th century in Spain.[92] This treatise was a conversation between Julien of Toledo and Idalio, Bishop of Barcelona. To this effect, Julian tried to provide answers to trending questions that dealt with the "situation of the souls of the deceased between the death of each individual and the resurrection at the end of time."[93] This work had great influence in the Middle Ages and beyond as scholars brought to the fore two principles of systemization: the historical/biblical system of Hugo of St Victor and the ideological type of systemization of Peter Abelard.[94] Studying theology should be understood as an ongoing exposition of salvation history. This way of looking at the study of eschatology makes some reasonable point concerning the "temporally ultimate."[95]

The "temporally ultimate" explains that everything should be viewed as an explanation or understanding of salvation history; even the temporal-ephemeral-transitory world has an eschatological end. Unlike the nihilists, who believe that life ends in nothingness, the temporally ultimate

---

Eschatology ed. Jerry L. Wall (Oxford University Press: New York, 2008), 23-39.

[91] Ibid.

[92] Pozo, *Theology of the Beyond,* xxi.

[93] Pozo, *Theology of the Beyond,* xxii.

[94] Pozo, *Theology of the Beyond, xxiv.*

[95] Pozo, *Theology of the Beyond,* xxiv.

purports something posterior to human life and history. To this effect Vicki Petrakis asserts that the "biblical account of the human person has its basis in how Irenaeus talks about the Trinitarian God, as *creatio ex nihilo*, vested in what he creates; not on account of God needing creation but because Irenaeus sees in this creative act God's *economia* and salvation entrenched."[96] Thus, the man that God creates *ex nihilo* does not end in nihilism because in God's creative act and *economia* his purpose is salvation for man. Petrakis further clarifies this purposefulness:

> Without God's imprint in the human makeup...man's access to God's divine life and God's access to man diverge. The matter from which man is initially formed in Irenaeus' theology presents more than divine dispensation. It is divine creation coexisting in the magnitude of God's identity and Being, and the blueprint for man's salvation in the Holy Spirit.[97]

This quote clearly stipulates that our existence in the temporal world has an ultimate effect, our salvation, which is why God created us. Thus, unlike the nihilists who attribute everything to chance and a life that ends in nothingness, Vicki Petrakis and Candido Pozo show that man's living beyond this world is due to the fact that man has God's imprint as the creature who has access to God's divine life. The metaphysical principle

---

[96] Vicki Petrakis, "The Plasma as Salvation History in St Irenaeus of Lyons," in *Phronema*, vol. 34 (2019), 103-123.

[97] Petrakis, "The Plasma as Salvation History in St Irenaeus of Lyons," in *Phronema*, vol. 34 (2), (2019), 103-123.

quidquid recipitur ad modum recipientis recipitur[98] means that I cannot move myself, so therefore there must be a prime mover. Life, therefore, has an eschatological purpose. The world cannot explain itself, so it must need an immanent principle of sufficient reason; but, the lack of technical vocabulary or refusal to use it makes scientists, and others, to think they can move themselves.

Yet the title of the first tract on eschatology by Julien of Toledo has much to teach. *Prognosticon futuri saeculi*, when considered from the point of view of prognosis, "raises the idea of a prior knowledge, doubtlessly arising from the data of revelation, of the future age that has not yet arrived."[99] This title brings out a clear connotation of prognostication in several instances in the New Testament. For instance, "the sons of this age marry but the ones in the age to come do not marry" (Luke 20:34-35). Another passage is, "whoever sins against the Son of Man will be forgiven but whoever speaks against the Holy Spirit will not be forgiven, either in this age or in the age to come" (Matthew 12:32). Finally, Jesus says, "Truly I say to you, there is no one who has left house or brothers or sisters or mother or father or children or lands, for my sake and for the sake of the gospel, who will not receive a hundredfold now in this time, houses and brothers and sisters and others and children and lands, with persecutions, and in the age to come eternal life" (Matthew 10:29-30).

Eschatological hope starts now, and it is lived now, but the ultimate hope is the coming kingdom. Thus, the last things

---

[98] "Whatever is received is received in the manner of the giver."

[99] W. Bauer, Briechisch-deutsches Wörterbuch zu den schriften des Neuen Testaments und der ubrigen urchristlichen Literatur, 5t ed. Berlin 1958 54ff.

are not only viewed from the perspective of the temporally ultimate but the ideological as well, which employs the *exitus-reditus* schema. In this schema, the reality of the history of salvation proceeds from "God to creation, which itself proceeds from God [*exitus*]."[100] The work of the *reditus* begins in the incarnation in which Christ redeems and makes the church a sacramental Church.[101]

Amid these developments, the term "eschatology" comes into the 20th century, a coinage of Protestant theologian K.G. Bretschneider.[102] For Bretschneider, this term meant what is normally the treatises on final or the last things. Later Oberthür, a Catholic theologian, adopted it in his biblical anthropology as a synonym for the "last things."

The above paragraph points to the fact that the meaning and scope of eschatology ought to be the kingdom of God without losing sight of its *already-ness* in this age since it concerns the relationship of faith to the last things.[103] This faith must be lived out in this world in preparation for the last things when we die. Therefore, the attraction of those who believe and propagate secular existentialism, or the Marxist opiate, should be shunned. They have not understood the theology of life after death and so continually deceive themselves of what it is and how to live in this world. With such

---

[100] Pozo, *Theology of the Beyond*, xxvi-xxvii.

[101] Ibid

[102] He coined this term in his earlier work and it gradually gained grounds as many theologians starting using it in their writings. K.G. Bretschneider, "Versuch einer systematischen Entwickelung aller" in *der Dogmatik vorkommenden Begriffe* (Leipzig 1805), 476.

[103] Jean Carmignac, *Les Dangers de l'eschatologie* (Paris: Letouzey et Anè, 1978), 93.

misunderstandings, a biblical understanding of eschatology becomes a prerogative following this scope and meaning.

2.2. Biblical Basis of Life after Death

The International Theological Commission teaches that the Bible is the soul of theology: "Theology in its entirety should conform to the scriptures, and the scriptures should sustain and accompany all theological work."[104] This is true of theology in general and eschatology in particular. The centrality of the promise of Jesus that he will come again in biblical eschatology becomes what distinguishes biblical eschatology from every form of "predictive futurism."[105] It is not predictive but is a promise which Jesus made, and it is verifiable in the Scriptures. Misunderstandings about Scriptures cause man not to be perceived in his undivided unity as God's creature with an eschatological purpose.

God of the Old Testament was known as the God who conquered in battles and wars in defense of the Israelites, his chosen people. As the conqueror, the Lord said he will put all his enemies under his feet (Psalm 110) as he had been doing for them in battles and wars, but the last enemy to be destroyed was death (1 Corinthians 15:26). Death's destruction here is not nihilistic; death is conquered by Christ's death and resurrection. This will happen on the "Day of the Lord"[106] or the "Day of Yahweh." In this light, Bill Arnold

---

[104] International Theological Commission, *Theology Today: Perspectives, Principles and Criteria*, n. 21.

[105] John Webster, *Word and Church, Essays in Christian Dogmatics* (Edinburgh: T&T Clark, 2001), 275.

explains that the Israelites continually spoke about Yahweh as the creator and protector of the Israelites, and consistently took center stage saving and protecting them from their enemies. God therefore established his dominion and Israel was his "treasured possession."[107] Therefore, the eschatological framework of Israel which hinges on the Day of Yahweh can

> be traced along a historical continuum in the narration of redemptive history, beginning with the ancestral promises of Genesis…since neither the numerical extent of the progeny as a great nation nor the geographical extent of the land promised became a reality in the lives of the ancestral generations, the promises themselves are by definition projected into the future.[108]

This projected future is the "Day of the Lord." This day is the eschatological hope in which the Israelites, and now all, will either inherit that kingdom which God has prepared for us or be damned because there is a survival of the psyche as we can infer from the above (Wis. 1).

Johan Fischer says the book of Wisdom is "intended to be a book of consolation for pious Jews, and especially for those persecuted on account of their faith."[109] Its purpose

---

[107] Bill T. Arnold, *Old Testament Eschatology and the Rise of Apocalypticism*, 25.

[108] Bill T. Arnold, *Old Testament Eschatology and the Rise of Apocalypticism,* 25.

[109] J. Fischer, *Das Buch Der Weischeit, in Echter Bibel*, Vol. 4 (Würzburg: 1959), 723.

makes salient the eschatological conception expressed in the soul, whose immortality is being preached. The just, when they die, possess this immortality immediately: "the souls of the just are in the hands of God and no torment will ever touch them" (Wisdom 3:1). Verse 3 continues, "they are at peace." Chapter 5 verse 15 says, "the righteous live forever and their reward comes from the Lord." These verses are eschatologically dense, as they show that life does not end at death. Those literalists and fundamentalists who reject the scriptures for their personal gains never quote these verses.

The books of Job and Qoheleth offer a critique against the long-established connection between "action and destiny." In Qoheleth, all is vanity as "he is ready to live without meaning and not to trust in a meaning as yet unknown."[110] He knows that life can become a crisis. On the other hand, Job's experiences show a trust in God as the redeemer over and against a senseless God. In these texts, Joseph Ratzinger sees a "glimmer of hope for an abiding life to come,"[111] though the nature of such a hope is unknown. These, therefore, recount a finality of death as not the end of life, but the continuation and rebirth of new life.

Daniel 12:2 falls in the genre of "martyr literature," giving us a new assurance to life and a way of enduring death. Verse 2 states that "many of those who sleep in the dust of the earth shall awake, some to everlasting life, and some to shame and everlasting contempt." Ratzinger says that Daniel 12 forms the clearest formulation of life after death that the

---

[110] Ratzinger, *Eschatology: Death and Eternal Life*, 78.

[111] Ibid.

Old Testament contains.[112] Glimpses of resurrection and the conquering of death are already prefigured in the Old Testament and continue to be fulfilled and developed in the New Testament.[113]

The New Testament preserves the basic thrust of the Old: "The martyrdom and raising to new life of the 'Just One,' par excellence, cloth in flesh and blood, in the vision of the author of Psalm 73 and the hope-filled confidence of the Maccabees," cannot be overlooked. The New Testament is viewed in synchronization with the Old, and Christ as the fulfilment and conqueror of death. His resurrection answers the cry of "troubled faith" in the face of death, the last enemy, finally conquered.[114]

The conquering of death is not in the light of the exact sciences and technical advances, as noted above, but in the manner that reconstructs the finality of death from any materialistic trivializations. Death, conquered by Christ, is life transformed. Death, Ratzinger affirms, "has vanished: only life remains."[115] Suffering, sickness, life, death, and life after death now gain a new meaning because "the God who personally died in Jesus Christ fulfilled the pattern of love beyond all expectations, and in so doing justified that human confidence which in the last resort is the only alternative to self-destruction [and so] the Christian dies into the death of Christ himself."[116] Human life, therefore, has meaning

---

[112] Joseph Cardinal Ratzinger, *Eschatology,* 90.

[113] There are more instances of the resurrection prefigured in the Old Testament but these will suffice.

[114] Ratzinger, *Eschatology: Death and Eternal Life,* 92.

[115] Ratzinger, *Eschatology: Death and Eternal Life,* 92.

[116] Ratzinger, *Eschatology: Death and Eternal Life,* 96.

because Christ's dying and rising gave it a different dimension that the exact sciences cannot explain; literalism cannot come close and any explanation leads to trivialization because of its rejection of faith and hope in the survival of the soul.

Christ's death and resurrection, therefore, forms the most undisputable and old account in the Gospels as a proof of the resurrection and the fact that we shall rise. The declaration of Ratzinger that "the heart of Christianity is the Paschal mystery of death and resurrection"[117] shows how central life is for the Christian, that God had to suffer ignominiously and die to give it meaning.

2.3. Christ's Resurrection, Hope for Our Resurrection

In the Creed, we profess that we believe in the resurrection of the body and life everlasting in articles 11 and 12 respectively. The resurrection of the body is Article 11 of the Creed, while life everlasting is found in in Article 12. These are hierarchical truths, summarizing the corpus of the Christian faith. Eschatological hope is not a recent idea. It has been formulated in the Church's faith and found in scriptures as evidenced by the death and resurrection of Jesus Christ.[118] The International Theological Commission writes that the Christian response to the "perplexities of people today, as indeed people of every age, has the Risen Christ as its foundation and is contained in the hope of the glorious future resurrection of all who are Christ's."[119] This is made possible

---

[117] Ratzinger, *Eschatology: Death and Eternal Life*, 92.

[118] *Catechism of the Catholic Church*, n. 989.

[119] International Theological Commission, *Some Current Questions in Eschatology*, 59.

since, in the same way as Christ took our likeness, we shall also enjoy his likeness in the resurrection of the body (1 Corinthians 15:49).

In the resurrection of the body, there is a difference between earthly bodies and heavenly bodies (1 Corinthians 15:40 ff). The body we possess now becomes a transformed body at the resurrection. In the analogy Paul presents, the body is sown perishable, but at the resurrection it is raised imperishable. It is sown in dishonor but raised in glory, sown in weakness but raised in power, and it is sown natural but raised spiritual (1 Cor. 15:42-44). Most importantly, these changes affect the same subject, the same individual. The Greek uses two words to make clear that it is the same person who becomes transformed. There is essential continuity between the body we have now and the transformed body after the resurrection. The Greek word that designates the earthly and risen body in v.44 is *soma*, which indicates continuity and an identity. The adjectives *psuchichon* and *pneumatichon* change in the two situations, but they affect the same subject.[120]

It must be noted that the resurrection of Christ, through whom we shall be resurrected, is not reincarnation. John Bowden categorically says that reincarnation, though it has been accepted by many, including Christians, has never been a Christian doctrine or teaching because it goes against the resurrection.[121] Reincarnationists believe the same life is brought back for purification purposes as the soul continues to seek total purification. This ideology is contradictory

---

[120] Pozo, *Theology of the Beyond,* 225.

[121] John Bowden, "Life after Death," *in Christianity: The Complete Guide*, eds. John Bowden et al, 2005, 706-710.

because it is based on a desire, as Lucky Dube sang, to fulfil that which was left undone in this world or to be purified. The poem of Emily Dickinson number 373 explains this in a better way. She says "The world is not a conclusion. A Species stands beyond-invisible, as Music but positive, as sound. It beckons, and it baffles. Philosophy do not know and through a Riddle, at the last sagacity, must go. To guess it, puzzles scholars. To gain it, Men have borne contempt of Generations and Crucifixion shown…Narcotics cannot still the Tooth that nibbles at the soul." Our future resurrection is an extension to humanity of the very resurrection of Christ.[122] Among the many causes for the increasing belief in reincarnation is the syncretism among different religions. At some point, the struggle for ecumenical dialogue tends to be destructive, as there are times when people with credulous minds easily are misled. For instance, during most ecumenical services, one religion often dominates the other, and in my ecumenical encounters, the Catholic aspect seems to be diminished and the other religions take the upper hand.[123]

Another point that the resurrection is not impossible is the raising of Lazarus from death. God, in raising Lazarus from the dead, shows his power in raising us too from the dead at the appointed time. Augustine beautifully expounds

---

[122] Congregation of the Doctrine of the Faith, *Recentiores Episcoporum Synodi*, 2, 941.

[123] During an ecumenical prayer service at Saint Mary's Seminary and University in the Fall of 2018, I left with the impression that it was not all ecumenical because I thought the prayers of the various churches and ecclesial communities participating would be synchronized so that non were left out, but to my surprise, it was more about the others without much attention to other communities. In this regard, I would propose that such services rather be deeply biblical to curb such excesses, or they should be carefully synchronized as to cause everyone experience what they are used to.

on this when he says that God absolutely knows from where to raise that which he created.[124] In a larger context, this shows the power of God over the "Superman" of Nietzsche, as man's reliance on God cannot be understated. Man's claim to be the Superman makes him misuse his freedom, thereby rendering him unfree, a slave to self and a slave to necessity.[125] Therefore, when Nietzsche claims the existence of the Superman, he becomes "unfree" because he is no longer a participant in the redemptive power of God as to be raised to new life, but is a slave to his own necessity which necessitates his damnation and eternal punishment, rather than a glorious resurrection to eternal bliss.

2.4. Resurrection of the Flesh

A basic distinction needs to be made; given that the terminology of "body" is that of the Nicene-Constantinopolitan Creed and the Athanasian Creed. In Eastern Greece, Egypt, and the Council of Toledo the resurrection of the "flesh" was mentioned. Interestingly, in 5th century Gaul it was recorded that before the consecration of bishops, they had to publicly promise their belief in the resurrection of the "flesh."[126] How, then, can we reconcile these assertions considering the Creed and the Pauline assertion? Ratzinger notes that people have generally arrived at a modicum that the resurrection of the "flesh" must, in some way, involve that of the "body." However, the *Catechism of the Catholic Church* offers a succinct understanding of the term "flesh" in the context of the resurrection: "The term 'flesh' refers to man in his state of

---

[124] Augustine, *De Civitate Dei*, (Tonholti: Brepols, 1955), 22,20,2.

[125] Collin E. Gunton, *Intellect and Action: Christian Theology and the Life of Faith,* (Edinburg: T&T Clark 2019), 179.

[126] Ratzinger, *Eschatology: Death and Eternal life*, 133-136.

weakness and mortality. The resurrection of the flesh (the literal formulation of the Apostles' Creed) means not only that the immortal soul will live on after death, but that even our mortal body will come to life again."[127] This, therefore, clarifies the difficulty posed in Paul; flesh is weak, but after the resurrection both the immortal soul and body will live on. Most importantly, the *resurrection* and the *incarnation* are correlative terms. Thus, any conceptions of death that does not have this admit this correlation runs into problems with the deposit of faith and the hierarchy of truths, thereby trivializing death.

Origen further expatiates on the resurrection of the body by referring to two unique principles of the body; namely, that matter which is the physical body is ever in constant flux, thus failing to retain its full identity, and that matter thus becomes the persistent form the individual gives himself. However, "the risen body cannot lie in what is ever-changing [thus] the final state our bodies will attain will not be based upon the caprice of earthly circumstance."[128] At the resurrection, we shall have *essential, ideal* bodies which Paul calls "glorified bodies," and this is possible because we have immortal souls.

2.6. The Immortality of the Soul

In his *Professio Fidei* [Profession of Faith], Paul VI affirms the body-soul anthropology of humanity, saying that the soul is spiritual and immortal.[129] By immortality, we mean that man's soul is aeviternal, having a beginning but not an

---

[127] *Catechism of the Catholic Church*, n. 990.

[128] Ratzinger, *Eschatology: Death and Eternal Life*, 177.

[129] Paul VI, *Professio Fidei,* (Libreria Editrice Vaticana, 1998), n.8.

end. This emphasizes that life with Christ is one that "not even death can destroy," but one that goes forever.[130] This means that man is a duality and not a dualism because according to dualism, the body is extrinsic to the soul whose successive existence assumes an altogether different body.[131] With duality, it is the same body that is reunited with the soul after the resurrection. This spiritual element in man is immortal, subsists after death, endowed with consciousness and freewill, making the human "I" to subsist devoid of the complement of its body between death and the resurrection.[132] Unlike the materialists, especially Feuerbach, who sees the survival instinct as a sign of utter destruction at death, life does not end at death. At death there is a temporal separation of the body from the soul, whose reunion will take place at the glorious resurrection.

Therefore, when Karl Marx sees religion as a promised betterment beyond this world that never gets materialized, he is mistaken. Man's search for a betterment goes beyond this life because he is immortal. Despite the material accumulation, the soul needs to be catered for because we live not solely for this earth, but for the world to come. As important as a revolutionary struggle is for the world, anyone who loses sight of the world beyond is mistaken. Marx, therefore, sees man only as material. As beings created by God who has us in his memory, we shall return to him. Even in suffering, we are no less immortal, so for Marx to say that

---

[130] Joseph Ratzinger, *Eschatology: Death and Eternal life*, 147.

[131] International Theological Commission, *Some Current Questions in Eschatology*, 86.

[132] Pozo, *Theology of the Beyond,* 250.

because Jesus suffered, he is truly the son of man[133] and not the son of God, is a misunderstanding. Suffering does not make one less in the eyes of God; war-torn and poverty-stricken nations are affected by man's selfishness and wickedness in harnessing the resources of the earth for their desired end and not for the good of mankind. Whether one adheres to the schema of Karl Marx or lives in in the poverty-stricken world, his theory seeks to dethrone religion, our eschatological goal is to savor eternal bliss with God.

We have sought to reconstruct the finality of death from the materialistic trivializations rampant in the world today, in order words, to state that man is immortal. By immortality, we mean that he is aeviternal, having a beginning but not an end. The emphasis is that life with Christ is one that "not even death can destroy" but one that goes forever.[134] As a created being, "man is destined for a relationship that entails indestructibility."[135] We are created for greatness, and we only need to work at achieving it.

In this respect, Ratzinger's contribution to the question of eschatology stands against any materialistic trivializations. He maintains two claims: relationship or communion and beings in God's memory. To the first, he maintains that seen from above, man's distinguishing mark is "his being addressed by God, the fact that he is God's partner in dialogue, the being called by God. Seen from below, this means that man is the being that can think of God, the being

---

[133] Bob White, *Jesus, the Complete Guide* (London: Continuum, 2020), 168.

[134] Ratzinger, *Eschatology: Death and Eternal life*, 147.

[135] Ratzinger, *Eschatology: Death and Eternal Life*, 154.

opened onto transcendence."[136] The point at this juncture is not whether he ever thinks of God, but that he is capable of doing so even if he never ever makes use of this capacity. Man is a being in relationship, vertically and horizontally, and so creating solutions or reasons that sever him from the finality of death become a call for concern. Materialistic trivializations of death have become a contemporary way of shunning God's dialogical call and capacity imbued in man to use for his betterment. As a being ordered to God, "creaturely being and trinitarian being-unveils its final countenance as love in the death and Resurrection of Jesus Christ,"[137] since man possesses a spiritual soul whose meaning is that he is a being created and loved by God, who continually calls him for dialogue or relationship with him that will not end in death, as opposed to the forces that make trivial those moments of genuine dialogue. In God's wish, a relationship is first and foremost because we are in God's memory.

We live, Ratzinger stipulates, because we are in God's memory, and our continued existence is because we are inscribed into God's memory where we are not a shadow, nor are we just recollection. We forever remain in God's memory, and this means we are alive.[138] Memory is not simply recollection, and God's memory is perfect unlike, our own memory. Augustine, according to Etienne Gilson, refers to the mind's knowledge of itself since the mind cannot be separate from self-knowledge, whereas our actual knowledge

---

[136] Ratzinger, *Introduction to Christianity* (San Francisco: Ignatius Press, 2004), 354.

[137] Nicholas J. Healy, *The Eschatology of Hans Urs von Balthasar: Being as Communion* (MA: Oxford University Press, 2005), 211.

[138] Ratzinger, *Eschatology: Death and Eternal Life, 20.*

(*cogitatio*) does not always have to do with our minds. Therefore, "the mind is what the divine model is because it was made in its image, and for this reason the influence of the eternal reasons along with the latent memory the soul has of itself are both needed if it is to discover itself as it is."[139] Thus, our minds in relation to the divine mind are limited, but this tells us what the perfect mind, God, is.

2.7. Eternal Life, Our Eschatological Goal

The metaphysical principles of causality teach that the final cause is the first to be imagined but the last to be realized. Applying this to human existence, Peter Kreeft says that "the story of any individual or community gets its meaning, point, and purpose from its end. So to know what kind of story we are in, to know what is the "meaning of life," we must know our end."[140] This knowledge of our end, Kreeft argues, is both logically coherent and innate in us as we always yearn for "something more" than this world.

This "something more" is not limited to the survival instinct that Feuerbach sees as the only reason for no immortality and life after death, but "a real life everlasting" which alone makes sense to our deep and innate and universal desires, which this world cannot fulfil.[141] In this regard Augustine claims, "Thou hast made us for thyself, and our hearts are restless until they rest in thee."[142] These

---

[139] Etienne Gilson, *The Christian Philosophy of Saint Augustine* (Rhode Island: Cluny Media Edition, 2020), 324-325.

[140] Peter J. Kreeft, *Catholic Christianity: A Complete Catechism of Catholic Beliefs based on the Catechism of the Catholic Church* (CA: San Francisco, Ignatius Press, 2001), 142.

[141] Peter J. Kreeft, *Catholic Christianity,* 142.

[142] Augustine, *The Confessions,* 5.

desires come from within and are not mere externals like power, the desire to become the Superman, food, drink, and wealth, which Karl Marx and Friedrich Nietzsche teach.

Another reason to logically assert the existence and longing for eternal life is that our eschatological goal is love. Love, therefore, has an eschatological dimension because love sees people as valuable in themselves, indispensable, and cannot be replaced. Gabriel Marcel makes an excellent point in this respect. He says love is a paradigm of communion and so it is an "essential ontological datum."[143] To say that I love you "is to say you, you in particular, will not die."[144] Love, therefore, has an eschatological dimension and can be seen as a realized eschatology. As realized eschatology, "life will be much better lived here in relation to the heavenly reality. If death ends all, if life treats these indispensable persons as if they were dispensable and disposable things, then life is an outrageous horror. No one can live in the face of death knowing that all is utter emptiness."[145] Therefore, when Nietzsche preaches love of self and the Superman, he goes against the instinct of love, which seeks harmony and peace rather than division. Because of this end, our lives continue to be lived in this light because death is not an end to man.

The Church teaches that at death, we either enter everlasting life, damnation, or purgatory (Catechism of the

---

[143] Gabriel Marcel, *Homo Viator: Introduction to the Metaphysics of Hope* (Indiana: St. Augustine's Press, South Bend, 2010), 147.

[144] Gabriel Marcel, *Homo Viator: Introduction to the Metaphysics of Hope* (Indiana: St. Augustine's Press, South Bend, 2010), 147.

[145] Ingmar Bergman, *The Seventh Seal*, Accessed at https://www.academia.edu/29162681/Bergmans_The_Seventh_Seal on October 10th 2021.

Catholic Church). Once we follow the innate desires for a good end and the teachings of the Church, we die to live. In John 11:25, Jesus says, "I am the resurrection and the life." We, too, are raised to this life in Christ who died so that we can have life abundantly. To this, Fulton J. Sheen wittingly states,

> If Jesus had said: I am the resurrection, without promising to bestow spiritual and eternal life, there would have been only the promise of reincarnation into successive layers of misery. If he said: I am the Life, without saying, I am the Resurrection, we would have merely the promise of our continued discontents." [When he combines the two, the effects are totally mystical, an affirmation that] "in Him was a life which, by dying, rises to perfection; therefore, death was not the end, but the prelude to a resurrection in the newness and fullness of life.[146]

In this, Sheen stresses the importance of life which is our ultimate end. Our striving for life everlasting is not an illusion or a blind following because Jesus, who is the way, the truth, and the life (John 14), categorically says he is the resurrection *and* the life. This life is not a return to successive layers of misery but a mystical effect that in Christ was life which "by dying, rises to perfection."

Life is a gift from God in this world which should logically lead to eternal life in the world to come. The life God breathed on man at creation is continued to eternal life.

---

[146] Fulton J. Sheen, *Life of Christ* (New York: McGraw-Hill Book Company, Inc., Toronto, 1958), 265.

Elements of this eternal life when it attains its plenitude abound in Scripture.

2.7.1. Intimacy with God

When the Scriptures say that God will take the righteous to himself, this is an expression of intimacy with God. For instance, Philippians 1:23 says, "my desire is to depart and be with Christ." This 'being with Christ' is intimacy with God. Practicing or living in intimacy with God is not something wholly in the future. It starts here on earth and its full consummation is eternal life, where we enjoy eternal bliss. Jim Hampton, in *Sacred Time, Living in the Presence of God*, says that to live in God's presence is first and foremost a discipline whereby one recognizes dependence on God, and then strives every day to grow in my love of him as one continually unites with him in prayer, meditation, , silence, solitude, service, and worship.[147] Life should be lived in balance with God as the focal point as we long for his kingdom here on earth. Thus, the stance of futuristic eschatologists like Moltmann and Pannenberg or presentism eschatologists is one-sided and should be rejected. If eschatology, or the struggle for intimacy with God, is something of the future, then one can live in any manner here on earth with the hope that he or she could steal heaven like the good thief. Another erroneous view is that there is intimacy with God which is just a reward for the life lived here. In this case, the present is not seen as meaningful intimacy with God but only a preparation for that future intimacy. In this light, *apokastasis* is reinforced, as many think that at the end they will all go to heaven irrespective of whether they lived good lives or not. The

---

[147] Jim Hampton and Amy Brothers, *Sacred Time Living in the Presence of God* (Missouri: Kansas City, 2009), 12-14.

church's understanding of intimacy with God rules out the ideas of amillennialism because it looks at this world as not fit for the rule of Christ. Such rejection of the world has compromised mankind of living eschatologically towards a glorious life with God.

On the other hand, if eschatology is seen as primarily present without any future, intimacy with God will not be complete since life comes to an end. Therefore, intimacy with God starts here on earth with the discipline of praying and developing a relationship with God, but it is consummated when we shall see the Lord face to face. A life without hope is not worth living, but a life that is totally centered on hope without any praxis for the present does not have meaning because we have intuitive vision of God.

2.7.2. Intuitive Vision of God

Two scriptural texts indicate that in eschatological discourse about our intuitive vision of God there is the "now" and the "then." These two sides give a balanced eschatological goal that begins here on earth and is consummated in heaven.

John says, "Dear friends we are children of God, and what we will be in future has not yet been known. But we know that when Christ appears, we shall be like him, for we shall see him as he is" (1 John 3:2). This tells us that we continually live eschatologically until we achieve that beatific vision. Given that Christ is the subject in both parts of the verse, he cannot be excluded, either here on earth or in heaven.

In 1 Corinthians 13:12, Paul says, "For now we see in a mirror dimly, but then face to face. Now I know in part; then I shall understand fully, even as I have been fully understood." To see dimly and then face to face speaks of the image of us in this world and in the beatific vision. The visible world, which we see dimly, then should be understood as the image of God. The knowledge of God in this world is "enigma," "obscure," and so it is only clear when we reach heaven.[148] Intuitive vision of God shows an eschatology that is not wholly present or future, but one that we live eschatologically until we see God face to face. In the case of a one-sided eschatology, the problem that Plato's prisoners face in the allegory of the cave will become the lot of humanity. In the allegory of the cave, the prisoners are chained to one position against a wall and cannot see anything behind them. The shadows they see projected on the opposite wall are just shadows of the *really-real* things behind them. They have grown so accustomed to these shadows that they think the shadows *are* the *really-real* things. Imagine some of them are freed from these bonds and they are led out to encounter the real essences of things. These are so bright for them that they cannot stand them. They almost go blind because the light is too much, and they quickly return to the cave.[149] Therefore, living eschatologically we begin to savor beatific vision of God as we continually develop intimacy with God until we finally see him *faciem ad faciem.*

2.8. Purifying State of Purgatory

After considering eternal life, which should be our desired destiny, it is important to examine other states of our Christian life, depending on how we live on this earth. The Church teaches that "eternal life begins immediately after death for the souls of the just who have nothing to be purged

---

[148] Pozo, *Theology of the Beyond,* 334-335.

[149] Plato, *The Republic* (MA: Harvard University Press, Cambridge, 1953), book VIII.

from. It is likewise defined that for the souls of those who die in actual moral sin, their damnation begins immediately."[150] When souls are not wholly purified but not in the state to enter eternal damnation, "a transitory state, distinct from the two definitive states of salvation and damnation," purgatory, completes the doctrine on intermediate eschatology. Here I will delve into the understanding of purgatory.

The Church has had several authoritative teachings on this doctrine, such as the Councils of Trent and Vatican II, as well as the Council of Florence. In the Council of Florence, the Church decreed,

> *If those truly penitent have departed in the love of God, before they have made satisfaction by the worthy fruits of penance for sins of commission and omission, the souls of these are cleansed after death by purgatorial punishments; and so that they may be released from punishments of this kind, the suffrages of the living faithful are of advantage to them, namely, the sacrifices of masses, prayers, and almsgiving, and other works of piety, which are customarily performed by the faithful for other faithful according to the institutions of the church.[151]*

This passage makes several salient points. First, it notes that nothing unclean enters heaven. Therefore, the souls in

---

[150] Pozo, *Theology of the Beyond,* 455.

[151] Council of Florence, https://www.ewtn.com/catholicism/library/ecumenical-council-of-florence-1438-1445-1461 (accessed October 5 2021).

purgatory are not eternally damned and so need the suffrages and good works of those on earth to assist them into eternal bliss. They need to be purified. However, this purification does not specify the length and time, so they need the prayers of the living.[152] Secondly, purgatory is a transitory state. The souls in purgatory will eventually go to heaven because it is a "continuation of a process of suffering which is necessary for souls seeking God, but this is a suffering which must inevitably end in perfect joy."[153] This state is different from souls in hell because of the surety that one day they will enter heaven, whereas the souls in hell are eternally damned.

The doctrine of purgatory is biblically based. The classic text is the book of Second Maccabees 12:43. The text says Judas Maccabeus took up a collection among his soldiers and sent it to Jerusalem for an "expiatory sacrifice." He did so because he had the resurrection of the dead in mind, since he expected the dead to rise again. Thus, this act made atonement for the dead that they might be freed from their sins. His action showed his belief in the resurrection. Secondly, this action means that those who died did not die in a "state of condemnation or enmity with God...[but] nevertheless, there was still something at fault in them, from which they had to be liberated."[154] Judas Maccabeus did this with the view of the resurrection so that they too could enjoy the resurrection, like every pious Jew. This text shows his

---

[152] John A. Hardon, *The Doctrine of Purgatory* (CA: Ignatius Press, San Francisco, 2001), 68.

[153] John Bowden et all, *Christianity, the Complete Guide* (London: Continuum, 2020), 1273.

[154] Pozo, *Theology of the Beyond*, 466.

understanding and appreciation of the power of prayer for purgation purposes.

This purgation or purification is different from the metempsychosists who believe souls will be returned to the earth to purify before they can enter heaven. There is no other bodily existence in this world when we die or when Christ will finally judge the living and the dead. Protestants rejected the doctrine of purgatory in part because they had rejected the canonicity of the books of Maccabees. Also, many of the protestants do not understand purgatory because of their teaching of sola fidei and so lack the biblical basis to believe it. Therefore, with the idea of justification by grace and no biblical evidence, they have no grounds for any belief in the doctrine of purgatory.

First Corinthians 3:12-15, that has some probative value about purgatory, is often discussed in this regard. Candido Pozo says that the text, while dealing with apostolic work, espouses an interesting doctrine in relation to the apostles.[155] Pozo notes that the text presents men who have built things of some value (v.12) on Christ as the foundation. He further observes that the day of judgment will show the solidity of each one's building.[156] Those whose buildings will stand the test will receive an immediate reward, but "if any man's work is burned up, he will suffer loss, though he himself will be saved, but only as through fire" (v.15). Here Pozo draws upon Fernand Prat, who understands the phrase, "suffering of loss," in this passage to mean, "they shall be saved but not without pain and distress, like people surprised by a sudden conflagration are saved by rushing through the

---

[155] Candido Pozo, *Theology of the Beyond*, 466-467.

[156] Candido Pozo, *Theology of the Beyond*, 466.

flames."[157] Therefore Pozo concludes that the pain and distress here is akin to the Church's understanding of purgatory as discomfort which does not last forever.[158]

2.9. Hell

John Paul II, in his catechesis on eschatology, writes, "hell indicates the state of those who freely and definitively separate themselves from God, the source of all life and joy."[159] This entails that our lives are not determined, but our free actions take us to either heaven or hell. Ideologies like determinism blur our eschatological vision and our authentic human existence as free and autonomous human beings created in the image and likeness of God. Where we go is determined by our free choices, not by God. In this light, Augustine says, "the God who created you without your cooperation cannot save you without your cooperation."[160] We must thus work out our salvation in fear and trembling (Philippians 2:12). Eternal damnation therefore "is not attributed to God's initiative because in his merciful love he can only desire the salvation of the beings he created. In reality, it is the creature who closes himself off to God's love. Damnation consists precisely in definitive separation from God, freely chosen by the human person and confirmed in death which seals his choice for ever."[161] Our "yes" or "no" to

---

[157] Fernand Prat, *The Theology of St Paul*, 11th ed., trans. John L. Stoddard (London: Newman Books, 1953), 97.

[158] Candido Pozo, *Theology of the Beyond,* 467.

[159] John Paul II, *General Audience*, Wednesday 28 July 1999, n. 3: www.vatican.va/holy_father/john_ii/audiences/1999/documents/hf_jp-ii_aud_28071999_en.html (accessed on October 9 2021).

[160] Augustine, *Sermon 163.*

[161] John Paul II, General Audience, Wednesday 28th July 1999, n.3.

God's will has an effect comparable to the *fiat* ("yes") of Mary in the Gospel, especially that the whole world stood still waiting for her answer. This means that despite the plans God has or wills for us, he never infringes on our freedom. Examples abound in scriptures. God could have prevented the Fall if he determined our actions, but because he created us free, the misuse of the freedom by our first parents brought suffering and pain into the world.

Many use the ideology of determinism to justify not working for salvation because they believe God has already determined whether or not they are saved. In response to this, the Blaise Pascal's "wager" provides interesting insights. He gives us two options. First, imagine that you strongly believe there is no God, and you live your life in that light. Then you die and discover there is a God after all. You have everything to lose. On the other hand, imagine you believe there is God, and you live everyday knowing there is God in the world to come. If you die and there is God, you have everything to gain and even if there is no God, you have nothing to lose.[162] Therefore, it is important to live like there is God. To the determinists who do not think there is God, the wager argument is a call to be alert rather than enter eternal damnation.

This wager argument equally counteracts the eschatological skeptics who think there must be a proof before something can be known to exist. They want to use the exact sciences to talk about matters of faith and revelation. In their doubts for the eschatological skeptics or laziness for the

---

[162] Blaise Pascal, *Le Pensee,* trans. W. F. Trotter (New York: Collier & Son, 1910), 1660.

determinists, they miss working for their salvation and continually work for their damnation.

In the Old Testament, specific instances show the preparation of the theme of hell which will surface in the New Testament, such as the human problem of outright evildoers thriving while good men languish in misery. In Psalm 39, the Psalmist sees "with indignation, the wicked man triumph."[163] Even though the Psalmist is not happy, he is afraid to utter mean words: "I will guard my ways, that I may not sin with my tongue; I will bridle my mouth, so long as the wicked are in my presence" (Psalm 39:1). As the Psalmist sees no change between the life of the wicked and the just, he prays for long life so that he may not depart in sadness. This similar scenario is repeated in the book of Job. Job suffers loss and illness but does not curse God, as some of his friends think he should. He remains true to God because he conceives his hope of seeing an "otherworldly solution" to his situation (Job 19:25).

2.9.1. Signification of *Sheol* in the Biblical Development of the Concept of Hell

In Isaiah 14, the King of Babylon in his greatness says he will ascend to the heights of the clouds as he makes himself the Most High, whereas others will be brought down to *Sheol*, the depths of the pit. Commenting on this, Johann Fischer writes that the king is carried to the deepest depth of *Sheol*. While in *Sheol,* the destiny of the ghosts is not the same for everyone, according to the prophets.[164] Proverbs 7:27 gives more meaning to the concept of *Sheol* as he

---

[163] Robert Tournay in La Sainte Bible of L'ecole Biblique De Jerusalem (Paris: Desclee, 1956), 690.

[164] Johann Fischer, Das Buch Isaias (I. Teil, Bonn 1937), 121.

mentions that lower stratum whereby sinners of the people of Israel, adulterers, and the foolish go. This assumes that there is a stratum for the just that is less deep, though still in *Sheol.*

In the mystical Psalms 16 and 49, the just man hopes to be taken out of this *Sheol,* and as he is taken up he will enjoy communion and intimacy with God, whereas the wicked will remain in *Sheol.* By this fact man is converted from a common abode of the dead into Heaven since the "spirits of the souls" of the just are raised to new life.[165] Daniel 12:2, with its prophecy of the resurrection, says that some shall go to everlasting life and others to everlasting contempt.

The New Testament opens with the announcement of eschatological chastisement by John in Matthew 3:10, who says that trees that do not bear fruits be cut down and thrown into the fire. The New Testament, therefore, affirms that the destiny of the just and the destiny of the wicked in the eschatological state are diverse as shown in Matthew 13:45: "So it will be at the close of the age. The angels will come out and separate the evil from the righteous." While the righteous go to eternal life, the damned or those on his left will be told to depart into the darkness (Matthew 25:30) where there will be weeping and gnashing of teeth.

Hell, therefore, is expressed with a *dolor sensibilis* (sensible pain) where there is an inextinguishable fire; Matthew, alluding to Isaiah 66, says it is better to lose a part of the body than to have the whole body go into Gehena (Hell). These development from the concept of *Sheol* in the Old Testament to Hell or Gehenna in many New Testament passages show that hell is a reality just as heaven is a reality.

---

[165] Helen K. Bond, *The Historical Jesus: A Guide for the Perplexed* (London: Continuum, 2020), 168.

The usage of graphic images shows how painful the loss of heaven can be, especially as hell is described as eternal damnation. However, this is not meant to scare us in this world but, as Von Balthazar says, when we read these grim pages about hell, rather than "forecasting a future destiny, the discourse on hell [should] serve to reflect humanity's present condition of turning from God."[166] This is important because hell is not created by God, but by sinners whenever they refuse a relationship with God or presume that God will save them irrespective of their good deeds. Therefore, Jesus' insistence on the existence of hell in several passages in Matthew should be taking as a warning that since the fall of Adam and Eve, human nature became forlorn, but Christ died for us so that we could be saved.

2.9.2. Conditionalism

Conditionalism is a further advance of the ideology of nihilism for the unjust at death, "whereas most Christians think all human beings are or will be immortal, conditionalists believe immortality is a gift God will grant only to those who meet the condition of being united in faith to the immortal One who redeemed them."[167] Anyone who does not die in a state of justice with God will be annihilated, either directly as a denial of the existence of hell or by means of a provisional hell.[168] The doctrine of hell does not suggest conditionalism.

---

[166] Jeannine Hill Fletcher, *Eschatology in Systematic Theology: Roman Catholic Perspective*, eds. Francis Schüssler Fiorenza and John P. Galvin (MN: Minneapolis, Fortress Press, 2011), 639.

[167] Christopher M. Date, "The Hermeneutics of Conditionalism: A Defense of the Interpretive Method of Edward Fudge" in *The Evangelical Quarterly*, 74 (January 1st 2018), 71-90.

[168] Pozo, *Theology of the Beyond*, 388.

Conditionalism teaches nihilism for the unjust at death, the nonexistence of hell for the unjust, and/or the existence of hell as a provisional place, not an eternal place of punishment. This view goes against the revealed truths contained in Sacred Scriptures; it is not true that the dead will be annihilated because they did not die at the state of grace with God. In physics, it is not possible for something that was there to be annihilated but it is surprising when scientists think the soul that has been there from the beginning can be annihilated. Spiritual things are impossible to be destroyed. Although hell cannot be destroyed, no one who goes to hell adds anything to God's greatness, but it is just because of the conditions our life choices take us to. The biblical record regarding hell and heaven shows there will be a place for the weeping and gnashing of teeth. The Bible does not say this place will only be temporal, or it does not exist; it is clear that it exists, and it is a truth of which Jesus himself spoke and against which he cautioned people. As Balthazar claims, even if one is uncomfortable with the truths about the fire of hell, the doctrine of hell should be viewed positively to serve as an orienting function that could be called the "spirituality of hell."[169] Once seen as an orienting function, then we will work hard not to die in a state of injustice since Christ himself stood, and continues to stand, alongside the sinner. Jesus takes no pleasure in the death of a wicked man, but rather lets him change his ways and live (Ezekiel 33:11). His divine kenosis, Balthazar continues, "witnesses him stooping to the lowest position of humanity in its sinfulness" upon the gibbet of the cross and after that descended to hell, thereby realizing the

---

[169] Hans Urs Von Balthasar, *The Mystery of Easter* (Edinburgh: T&T Clark, 1990), 23, 52.

agony and sin in the world.[170] The Church teaches that Jesus' descent to hell was to free the souls of the just who lived before him.[171] As we saw in the development of the word "hell," this was *Sheol* or the Hebrew "hades." There is no annihilation of God or of man after death and life does not end in nihilism. At death, the souls of the just enjoy eternal bliss and those who need purification go to purgatory, but the souls of the unjust are never annihilated, as they go to eternal punishment.

Another error about hell and its inexistence is the doctrine of universalism (*aposkastasis*). Being saved or being damned does not come without my cooperation, as Augustine intimated. By Christ's dying and rising he redeemed us, yet we must work for our salvation every day. Vatican II affirms that the Church has been sent to all nations so that she can be the universal sacrament of salvation.[172] Therefore, the catholicity of this salvation for the Church "consists in the fact that the universal offer of grace involves a relationship to the church on the part of every human person-a relationship, to be sure, that will vary according to the response each person makes to God's grace."[173] When conditionalists reject the possibility of hell or teach its temporality for purification purposes, they propound the doctrine of universal salvation.

---

[170] Hans Urs Von Balthasar, *The Mystery of Easter* (Edinburgh: T&T Clark, 1990), 23, 52.

[171] Sev Kuupuo, *He Descended In to Hell*, https://paloaltocatholic.net/news/he-descended-into-hell (accessed on September 23 2020).

[172] Paul VI, *Ad Gentes Divinitus*, ed. Austin Flannery (MN: Liturgical Press, 1965), n.1.

[173] Francis A. Sullivan, *The Church We Believe In* (NY: Paulist Press, 1988), 110.

In this light, hell is seen as a place where the purification of souls continues through successive incarnations. Both conditionalists and apokatastasists are neither true nor present sound doctrine.

In *Lumen Gentium*, the Church teaches that salvation subsists in the Catholic Church. The Council teaches what we profess in the Creed that the Church is One, Holy, Catholic, and Apostolic, which our savior after his resurrection entrusted to the care of Peter. This one Church, it further opines,

> *constituted and organized as a society in the present world, subsists in the Catholic Church, which is governed by the successor of Peter and by the bishops in communion with him. Nevertheless, many elements of sanctification and of truth are found outside its visible confines...they are forces impelling [her] towards Catholic unity.*[174]

There has been much debate about this statement since the Second Vatican Council. The words used before were *adest, est*-simply said, *Is the Catholic Church,* and so others are excluded by that very fact. The Congregation of the Doctrine of the Faith says *subsistit in* was adopted over *est* because *est* is exclusive to Catholics and so does not do justice to the *vestigia Ecclesiae* (elements of truth and sanctification found outside the Catholic Church, like the word of God, grace,

---

[174] Paul VI, *Lumen Gentium,* ed. Austin Flannery (MN: Liturgical Press, 1965) n. 8.

71

some sacraments, and the theological virtues).[175] Many
misleading and leftist positions have been taken by
theologians in this regard.[176] But the Church means that "they
derive their efficacy from the very fullness of grace and truth
entrusted to the Catholic Church."[177]   Both
Lumen Gentium and *Unitatis Redintegratio* take the
theologically and rationally satisfied ecumenical position given
that Jesus in John 17 had prayed for the moment when all will
be one as the Father is one. Therefore, other churches and
ecclesial communities, though they suffer from defect, cannot
be deprived of their importance in God's mystery of salvation.
These members receive salvation because of the fullness of
grace and sanctification present in the Catholic Church.[178] In
and by itself, *subsistit in* expresses two concepts worthy of
note:

*a past and ever-present ecclesiological reality,
namely the indefectibility of the Church that is fully*

---

[175] Joseph Cardinal Ratzinger, "Congregation for the Doctrine of the
Faith," in *Responses to Some Questions Regarding Certain Aspects of the
Doctrine on the Church* (Washington D.C.: USCCB, 2012).

[176] The case of Francis Sullivan S.J in his *Quaestio Disputata* is not to
be taken seriously because it is misleading. His comment contains a lot of
inconsistencies to the Catholic doctrine on *Subsistit in*. He moves towards
philological and linguistic analysis of statements uttered by Ratzinger, the
Congregation for the Doctrine of the Faith and other theologians but among his
greatest errors is the fact that the Church maintains classical Latin as her official
language because modern languages change and develop. Instead of looking at
the meaning as derived from the Latin and its present usage, he uses the
commentary of *Subsistit in* in the 80s forgetting that German change and
progress. A full reference of this is found in Francis A. Sullivan, *Quaestio
Disputata*: The Meaning of *Subsistit in* as explained by the Congregation for the
Doctrine of the Faith and Further Thoughts on the Meaning of *Subsistit in.*

[177] Paul VI, *Unitatis Redintegratio,* n.3. Also, confer, Congregation for
the Doctrine of the Faith, Declaration, *Dominus Iesus*, n. 16.

[178] *Unitatis Redintegratio*, nn. 3-4.

assured-by the mercy of God-in the Catholic Church…with regards to the future the necessary moral and dogmatic progress that all the Churches and ecclesial communities must make, through dialogue, in order to converge, each one by its own path of progress into the full unity that, once attained, will enrich them all.[179]

Therefore, when the conditionalists say salvation is universal because hell does not exist cannot be adhered to because the Church is the universal sacrament of salvation and yet it does not refuse the existence of hell. Salvation subsists in the Catholic Church, so other ecclesial communities are saved in relation to the Catholic Church. The idea that universal salvation is a gratuitous gift, even for those who can be purified in hell, is faulty as hell is eternal; as the adage African adage goes, "there is no repentance in the grave." This point calls to the mind the *pro multis controversy.*[180]

---

[179] Benoit De La Soujeole, "Vocabulaire et notions a Vatican II et dans le magistere posterieur" *Revue Thomiste* 110, (2010), 245-273.

[180] "In the 1960s, when the Roman Missal had to be translated into vernaculars, under the responsibility of the bishops, there was a consensus among exegetes to the effect that the word —*many* in *Is* 53:11f. is a Hebrew expression referring to the totality, —all. It would follow that the use of the word —*many* in the institution narratives of Matthew and Mark is a Semitism and should be translated —*all*. This argument was also applied to the Latin text that was being translated directly, and it was claimed that —*pro multis* points beyond the Gospel narratives to *Is* 53 and should therefore be translated —for all. This exegetical consensus has collapsed in the meantime: it no longer exists. The account of the Last Supper includes the words: —This is my blood, the blood of the covenant, that is poured out for many (*Mk* 14:24; cf. *Mt* 26:28). This highlights something very important: the rendering of —*pro multis* as —for all was not merely a translation but an interpretation, a well-founded interpretation then as now, but an interpretation nevertheless, something more than a translation. (This is adapted from Pope Benedict XVI's letter to the President of the German Bishops' Conference, 14/4/2012.- adaptation is mine)

Ratzinger rejects the translation "for all" because to him, *pro multis* is not *pro omnibus.* It is worth noting that "for all" is the literal translation. Ratzinger draws this conclusion from three points: first, the universal saving will of God. Second, God does not force anyone to be saved and finally, "for all" and "for many" are both found in Scriptures and in Tradition, each underlining a particular aspect in soteriology. "For all" therefore underscores the universal saving will of God, while "for many" underscores human freedom to accept or refuse the universal offer of salvation.[181] Ratzinger's conclusion, therefore, maintains his understanding of the interdependence of "for all" and "for many," and if "for all" is not understood as an indiscriminate apokatastasis, neither should "for many" be taken as a restrictive Jansenism since neither of the two expresses the whole. [182] Now let us look at the Parousia.

2.10. The Parousia

The term *Parousia* comes from Greek, and it means "to be present" or "to arrive." Its basic meaning was preserved during the Hellenistic age, but "from the 3rd century before Christ, the word begins to be used to speak about a solemn visit and a joyous and festive entrance of a sovereign especially during the visit to a province."[183] This concept had

---

Cfr. J. Sango, *Exploring Ratzinger's Inspiration Of Vicarious Representation In Biblical Imagery*, Unpublished Essay.)

[181] Ratzinger, *God is Near us: The Eucharist, The Heart of Life* (CA: Ignatius Press, 2003), 34-38.

[182] Jansenism is a heresy that denies freewill in accepting the use of grace. It asserts that God's role in the infusion of grace cannot be resisted and does not require human assent.

[183] Pozo, *Theology of the Beyond,* 65.

already appeared in the Old Testament, most notably in Daniel 7:13.

The idea of the *two* messianic arrivals tell us that the messiah had come already, and that he will come again. This announcement is made by the angels to the apostles on Ascension Thursday, "Men of Galilee, why do you stand looking into heaven? This Jesus who was taken up from you into heaven, will come in the same way as you saw him go into heaven" (Acts 1:11). This means that between his ascension and his second coming there is an intermediary time which for Luke is a time of mission and preaching of Christ to all. For John it is a time for the mystical possession of the messianic goods whose manifestation are reserved for the end times.[184] Thus, Christ's second coming, or the Parousia, is understood in contraposition to the first because in his first coming, he came to free us from sin, but his second coming will be to save those eagerly waiting for him.

The Parousia, therefore, is the second coming of Jesus Christ to judge the living and the dead (Nicene Creed). However, no one knows the hour nor the time (cf. Matthew 24:36). Therefore, theories like millennialism, postmillennialism, amillennialism, and dispensionalism go against the authentic teaching of the Parousia, namely, that his coming is not within any time frame. For instance, when Irenaeus places the return of the Lord after the appearance of the anti-Christ,[185] but prior to the millennium, this gives the Parousia a timeframe that we are not able to explain or state clearly. The appearance of the anti-Christ produces nothing

---

[184] Pozo, *Theology of the Beyond,* 72.

[185] Skevington A. Wood, "The Eschatology of Irenaeus," in *The Evangelical Quarterly* 41 (1969), 30-41.

but relativism in our world today. Many prophets have arisen and condemned others to be false prophets. In doing so, the prophets say the anti-Christ has already come, and the presence of many itinerant preachers is a sign that the anti-Christ has come, and that the world is coming to an end. It becomes difficult to determine which three and a half years are those when the anti- Christ have come.

Similar difficulties in understanding the Parousia properly have been found in the understanding of "a thousand years" in the book of Revelations 20. Unfortunately, some early Christian teachers like Justin, Papias, and Irenaeus expected "a literal thousand-year period of an earthly paradise when Christ and the saints would rule the nations and biblical prophecies about a transformed creation."[186] This literal interpretation continues to find merit among fundamentalists and evangelical Christians today as they think Christ will return before the great tribulation, raise believers who died and take all true believers to heaven. [187] After seven years, he will come to defeat the beast, false prophets and their armies and thereafter the Church will reign for a thousand years within an eternal bliss on earth.[188] As earlier stated, Peter Williamson affirms, "The Catholic Church rejects millenarianism, interpretations like dispensationalism that expect a visible earthly reign of Christ before the final judgment."[189] The kingdom of God will not come by any

---

[186] Peter S. Williamson, *Revelation: Catholic Commentary on Scripture* (Michigan: Baker Academics, Grand Rapids, 2015), 329.

[187] Thomas Ice and Kenneth L. Gentry Jr., *The Great Tribulation* (Kregel Publication, 1999), 146-147.

[188] Scofield C. Ingerson, *New Scofield Reference Bible* (NY: Oxford University Press, 1983), 1374. In this section, see the notes on 30:2-4.

[189] Peter S. Williamson, *Revelation,* 331.

political messiah or any progressivity (*CCC* 677) but only by God's victory over the final unleashing of evil (*CCC* 677). Christ's Parousia therefore cannot be taken literally, but it will come to pass.

In this chapter, I have examined the Church's understanding of life after death. We have seen that eschatology today has developed through progressive stages, and that the *term* is much recent than the *theology* of eschatology. Further, I examined the biblical understanding of the Resurrection against the contemporary biblical misunderstandings of eschatology. The centrality of Christ's resurrection as the source of our resurrection shows that Christ's resurrection is the basis of our resurrection and counteracts any reincarnationist theories. At the end, Christ will come again and judge the living and the dead, and the world will come to a definitive end. This time is not known to anyone, and so any millennial doctrine about a period of a thousand years of bliss or specific time in relation to Christ's coming is out of our understanding.

At this juncture, we delve into chapter three, which will explore the hermeneutical tools for understanding life after death as interpretive tools to this endeavor and the pastoral applicability for contemporary society.

if you are enjoying this book leave a review for the author on amazon Thank you!

CHAPTER THREE

HERMENEUTICAL TOOLS TOWARDS AN INTERPRETIVE AND PASTORAL APPLICABILITY TO CONTEMPORARY ESCHATOLOGICAL LIVING

In the preceding chapters, I have undertaken an understanding of the prominent theories about life after death as well as the Church's understanding about life after death. In doing this, it is clear that questions about theology in general, and eschatology in particular, do not have definitive answers, as in the case of scientific and secularistic tendencies. Therefore, an understanding of these prominent theories that have confused and converted many from an authentic eschatological belief and hope beginning in this life and transitioning to the life to come should not be undervalued; theologians should come up with sound rebuttals that will change this narrative. We live eschatologically and often times are unaware of this. So, it is the place of the theologian to be missionary to the unchurched, the derailed, and the unconverted. The task of the theologian/pastor is beautifully captured by the character of the clown in the 1968 novel *Secular City* by Harvey Cox as wittingly explained by Ratzinger in *Introduction to Christianity*. In the novel, a traveling circus in Denmark caught fire and the manager sent a clown, dressed in his costume and makeup, to solicit for help. The clown ran to the nearby village. The more he solicited, the more people laughed and had fun because to them, he was just doing his job, entertaining them, and attracting more people to the show. Unfortunately, the village burned. [190]

The story of the stage clown, Ratzinger notes, is the story of the theologians and pastors in the world plagued by conflicting theories about eschatology. Despite the continual preaching and avenues of actual graces that preachers continue to make available, many are still misled by these theories and secularizing tendencies that only life after death itself serves as an interpretive tool to overcoming this quagmire. There is much work for pastors in their task of evangelization to reimagine ways that will attract their audiences to the truths about eschatology, to be saved and not just be entertained, as was the case with the clown's pleading.

This chapter will delve into the hermeneutical keys toward pastoral applicability to unlock those facets of understanding and interpreting life after death in relation to the

---

[190] Harvey Cox, *The Secular City* (London: Pelican Books, 1968), 256 and Joseph Cardinal Ratzinger, *Introduction to Christianity*, 39.

prominent theories seen in Chapter One and the Church's understanding of life after death in Chapter two, as a means to reach everyone pastorally about living eschatologically in the sure hope of possessing eternal bliss won for us at the price of Christ's blood. This is important because, as evangelizers, it is hard to convince people against the end of earthly life, the awareness of which is lacking due to insufficient understanding of metaphysics. According to the metaphysical principle of causality, the final cause is the first to be thought, but the last to materialize. This means that everything passes through the material cause, the formal cause, and the efficient cause before the final cause. The number of unfinished projects, like road construction, unfinished doctrinal preparation, some un-started, or poorly completed projects around us tell us how hard it is to persevere on the eschatological course without a rational understanding to reach the final goal.[191] Despite the difficulty of this eschatological project for evangelizers and the evangelized, the importance of arriving at the final cause cannot be overstated. Therefore, this arduous task of eschatological evangelization needs tools to unlock and interpret the eschatological reality to effectively approach the problem in a way that is pastorally gratifying, enriching, and directed toward converting souls to right relation with God.

3.1. Hermeneutical Tools for Eschatological Living

The term "hermeneutics" comes from the Greek verb *hermeneuein,* meaning to "interpret," "understand,"

---

[191] Herman Reith, *The Metaphysics of St Thomas Aquinas* (Michigan: The Bruce Publishing Company, Milwaukee, 1958), 154-167.

"translate."[192] When eschatology or theology is referred to as hermeneutical, its essential meaning is understanding, interpreting, and translating the message to the understanding and application to those for whom it is intended. For instance, theology has always been devoted to the understanding and interpretation of the Bible given how far removed the message is from its original recipients and the cultures in which it is received today. This is further made difficult by the contemporary loss in metaphysics and things not evidential and experiential, like eschatology. Therefore, "we are most intensively engaged in hermeneutics when we ask ourselves how we understand our lives."[193] Hermeneutical tools for dissecting the nature of the eschatological life are an imperative for a balanced application to the lives of the faithful by evangelizers.

3.1.1. Acceptance of Revealed Truths

The Dogmatic Constitution of the Church (*Dei Verbum*) states that "in His goodness and wisdom God chose to reveal Himself and to make known to us the hidden purpose of His will by which through Christ, the Word made flesh, man might in the Holy Spirit have access to the Father and come to share in the divine nature."[194] Through this revelation, God has made known to mankind the hidden mysteries so that through this invitation, humanity can come to fellowship with him. There is no human knowledge without presuppositions, as "all human knowledge and all human language depend on an already built-in structure of understanding and

---

[192] Pierre Bühler, "Hermeneutical Theology," in *Christianity: The Complete Guide* (London: Continuum, 2005), 525

[193] Bühler, "Hermeneutical Theology," 525.

[194] Paul VI, *Dei Verbum*. n.2

judgment."[195] Thus, in our struggle and search for truth, we always presuppose that this truth already exists, unique and universal. "The Church, by means of the unique Gospel she preaches, and which, in time, is revelation for all men and for all time, can meet all essential needs of the human intelligence which is in history and open to the universal. The Church can purify this and give it perfection."[196] However, many people rarely afford her the opportunity. This is because the Church constantly stands against the currents in what is trending in the society, and so many find it important to be recognized as celebrities than to stand to live out the Gospel that the Church continue to preach in season and out of season.

This presents the difficulty of the rejection of revelation in eschatological assertions, not just the contemporary world, but successively seen at various stages of human history and development. There is a continuous rejection of revealed truths, thereby making it difficult for an eschatological hermeneutic to be understood, interpreted, and translated to make meaning in this life as a preparation for the life to come as intended by the "sovereign personal God [who] is the creator of the universe and the absolute source of meaning and value."[197]

Avery Dulles notes that some people do not want to accept revealed truths because revelation "does not appear

---

[195] International Theological Commission, *The Interpretation of Dogma*, 28.

[196] International Theological Commission, *The Interpretation of Dogma*, 28-29

[197] Carl F. H. Henry, "*The Priority of Divine Revelation*: A Review," in The Journal of the Evangelical Theological Society (March 1984), 77-92.

in the creeds" and "is not central in the Scriptures."[198] Supporters of the idea that revelation is not scriptural see the Scriptures as a work of literature whose goal is for humans to be obedient, and not as a communication of the divine that calls on our assent.[199] How can we obey or proclaim salvation by a God who has not made himself known, nor manifested himself as a savior? The Church teaches that the living and personal God 'directly' and 'objectively' made himself known by intelligible words, acts, and commands. His redemptive revelation is given once for all at definite times and places, and he continually makes himself known in nature, history, and the minds and consciences of man everywhere. Scripture further furnishes us with consistent and supernatural teachings in miracles and fulfilled in prophecy. As of now, the prophetic and apostolic divine revelation is already complete with the revelation of Jesus Christ (Hebrews 1:1), but the pre-eschatological, my concern in this paper, evidenced in Scriptures, serves as God's full and final revelation when he will come to judge the living and the dead.[200]

The rejection of revelation as a hermeneutical tool for contemporary eschatological living has appeared in several critical constructs. First, atheism, naturalism, and humanism explain all reality in terms of natural processes, which means that everything ends in nothingness. In the words of J.P. Mackey, revelation is a "metaphorical or mythical description"

---

[198] Avery Dulles, *Revelation and Reason* (PA: Westminster, 1964), 3.

[199] F. G. Downing, *Has Christianity a Revelation?* (London: SCM; Philadelphia: Westminster, 1964), 46.

[200] B.B. Warfield, *Revelation and Inspiration* (New York: Oxford University Press, 1927), 48.

whose disciples creatively postulate divine authority.[201] This rejection helps account for the prevalence of atheists in the world. The hermeneutical eschatology, therefore, calls for a belief and acceptance of revealed truth because Jesus Christ made himself known, and revelation shows the existence of life after death.

Second, determinists advance the theory that the transcendent character of divine revelation undermines human freedom to support their argument that everything has been determined by God; but determinists choose the lesser evil to them, which is to do away with revelation. In this respect, Karl Jaspers says, "I myself cannot but hold with Kant that if revelation were a reality, it would be calamitous for man's created freedom."[202] It must be noted that in eschatological living, revelation and freedom are not antithetical. When Jaspers rejects revelation as antithetical to freedom, he rejects the idea that in revelation God does not curtail man's freedom, but rather gives him the logical reasoning for his adherence. This can be attested by the fact that Christ's dying was for "all," but the "many" who will be saved (as noted in Chapter Two) are those who used their freedom to work for their salvation in fear and trembling.

Thirdly, Marx's view of religion as a mechanism employed by oppressive forces to suppress dissenters is backed by the denial of revelation. For Marx, since the final consummation of revelation is in the eschatological end, any talk about the Divine is merely a manipulation to keep people

---

[201] J. P. Mackey, *Problems in Religious Faith* (Dublin: Helicon, 1972), 19-21.

[202] Karl Jaspers, *Philosophical Faith and Revelation* (New York: Harper 1967), 8.

weak because God did not reveal anything. To this, it is important to note with Blaise Pascal that it is better to die and discover there is no heaven when one has prepared than to die and discover there was heaven, but one never prepared for it.

The acceptance of divine revelation as shown above still leaves much to be desired. Given that revealed truths are a hermeneutical tool to understanding contemporary eschatological living, it is important to continue to bring awareness to society about Jesus Christ, who is the fulfillment of revelation and who came to this world, suffered, died, and rose from the dead as the way that we shall follow. His revelation culminated in the eschatological consummation of the world with God, and so divine revelation remains the basis for understanding contemporary eschatological living.

3.1.2. Criteria for the Resurrection of the Dead

In the previous chapter, I examined Christ's resurrection as the basis of our resurrection in the Church's eschatological teaching in contrast with the theories about eschatology prominent in society. In this chapter, the argument will be pushed further to understand Christ's resurrection as a hermeneutical and interpretive tool towards understanding contemporary eschatological living. In this respect, we note that it is Christ's resurrection that gives us the hope that we shall rise, and that he who rose from the dead will give life to our mortal bodies to make them like his own in glory[203] because "that which is a growth in hope among

---

[203] John L. May, *Order of Christian Funerals with Cremation Rite* (NJ: Catholic Book Publishing Company, 2019), 116.

the chosen people has been realized in the resurrection of Christ."[204]

In 1 Cor. 15, Paul says that what he passes on to believers is of prime importance; he reports the account of Christ's suffering, death, resurrection from the dead, and the hope of our resurrection. This, in my understanding, becomes a hermeneutical tool for understanding contemporary eschatological living because those who have no understanding of the Bible do not know that the resurrection is of first importance, according to Paul, in understanding life and life after death. For instance, it is only because of Christ's resurrection that everything he taught and did made sense to the apostles and believers.

Verse 17 makes clear that if Christ had not been raised from the dead, our faith would be useless. In this light, Markus Vinzent says, "If Paul, our oldest witness of the Resurrection, is so adamant on the Resurrection and makes it the sticking point of Christian belief - 'your faith is useless' without it - how should the resurrection be anything else but the basis of Christian belief?"[205] Therefore, to properly understand eschatology today, a "hermeneutical resurrection" needs to be awakened whereby evangelizers are able to use the resurrection of Christ in its prime importance to show how important it is for faith in the resurrection to be known and lived. To this point, Wilhem Schneemelcher explains that the Pauline heritage of belief in the Resurrection faded over time

---

[204] International Theological Commission, *Some Current Questions in Eschatology,* 58.

[205] Markus Vinzent, Christ's *Resurrection in Early Christianity: and the making of the New Testament* (VT: Ashgate Publishing Company, Burlington, 2011), 10.

as many remained reluctant towards Easter stories, while others were totally quiescent and up to the mid-second century, Sunday celebrations did not have the Resurrection as the focal point, as it is today.[206] Although it has been rekindled in the Sunday celebrations and solemnities, the present has its own difficulties that evangelizers need to tackle. For instance, explaining the resurrection as far as reason will allow before supplementing it with faith cannot be taken for granted since advancements in science have produced a society that is more factual than "faith-tual." Therefore, theories that refuse the resurrection of the dead or teach a wrong life after death, such as reincarnation and nihilism, teach the wrong understanding of living eschatologically and trivialize this important belief in Christianity; they do not bring back a Resurrection 'Mania' seen in early Christianity that increased belief in God.[207] The Resurrection of Christ therefore remains a hermeneutical and interpretive tool to unlocking contemporary eschatological living as a preparation for communion with God.

3.1.3. Eternal Life as Communion with God in Christ

Communion with God in the life to come is another hermeneutical tool in understanding contemporary eschatological living. In the previous chapter, we saw that when one is taken out of *Sheol* in the mystical psalms, it is to enjoy communion with God, and being sent to *Gehena* severs

---

[206] This rediscovery of the importance of the resurrection in Sunday liturgies was begun by Marcion of Sinope. W. Schneemelcher, Wilhelm, 'Paulus in der griechischen Kirche des zweiten Jahrhunderts', ZKG 75 (1964): 1–20.

[207] Markus Vinzent, *Christ's Resurrection in Early Christianity: and the Making of the New Testament*, 111.

that communion. In this section, I will further explore how eschatological communion with God starts on this earth and is consummated in heaven.

Jerome Dollard writes that the kingdom of God in Jesus Christ is a call to us to *koinonia, liturgeia,* and *diakonia*: communion, worship, and service.[208] Our ongoing conversion to Jesus is a letting go of self and finding our identity through Jesus in a relationship of trusting love with God the Father, giving us the experience of a united people as brothers and sisters in one God.[209] If this is part of ascent for the human person, for God it is a way of humble condescension, of self-emptying (kenosis). This flows from the Holy Thursday ceremonies where Christ gives the *sacramentum*[210] that becomes the *exemplum*,[211] a gift that becomes a task. Correct and authentic communion in this life is seen in our willingness to serve one another and worship as a community. This entails that man is not *"homo homini lupus*-a wolf to man"[212]

---

[208] Jerome Dollard, *"Eschatology, A Roman Catholic Perspective"* in Review and Expositor (1964), 367-380.

[209] Jerome Dollard, *"Eschatology, A Roman Catholic Perspective"* in Review and Expositor (1964), 367-380.

[210] *Sacramentum,* or "gift," here refers to the whole of the mystery of Christ in which he draws close to us, enters us through his spirit, and transforms us. Given that this *sacramentum* truly —cleansed us, renewing us from within, it also unleashes a dynamic of new life. (cf. Joseph Cardinal Ratzinger, *Jesus of Nazareth,* vol. II, 62)

[211] *Exemplum* or task here is the command to do as Jesus has done. This is not a mere moral appendix to the mystery of Christ. It follows from the inner dynamic of the gift with which the Lord renews us and draws us into what he is. To become a Christian then is primarily a gift, which unfolds in the dynamic of living and acting in and around the gift. (cf. Joseph Cardinal Ratzinger, *Jesus of Nazareth*, vol. II, 62)

[212] Thomas Hobbes, *On the Citizen*, eds. Richard Tuck and Michael Silverthorne (Cambridge: Cambridge University Press, 1998) 3.

as Thomas Hobbes emphasizes, and that living eschatologically is already a prerequisite in this life for the life to come, where true communion with God will be consummated.

This consummated communion is the final and perfect communion with the Triune God, when and where salvation means "union with Christ and being adopted as sons and daughters of the Father in the incorporating communion of the Holy Spirit."[213] This understanding of salvation as communion with the Triune God has two implications. First, we only see and commune with the Triune God if we justify ourselves in the "logic of grace" by living in the manner that God has revealed to us through his own revelation. Second, we commune with the Triune God by living in the presence of God's revealing light, accepting our sinfulness and receiving grace.[214] This means that those who have chosen the dictum "Christ died for all" but do not freely choose to work for their salvation because they think they have been determined are freely choosing not to commune with God at the end of their pilgrim journey. The communion perspective of living in the "logic of grace" relates the "entire sanctification to the Triune fellowship and salvific mission."[215] Thus, interpreting, translating, and shedding more light on the eternal communion with God is important in correcting theories like scientific materialism that teach that everything is material.

---

[213] Dick O. Eugenio, *Communion with The Triune God: The Trinitarian Soteriology of T.F. Torrance* (United Kingdom: James Clarke & Co, Cambridge, 2014), 156.

[214] Eugenio, *Communion with The Triune God,* 157.

[215] Susan B. Carole, *Called to Communion: A Paradigm Shift in Holiness Theology* (OR: Wipf and Stock Publishers, Eugene, 2013), Chapter 5.

3.1.4. A Correct Basis for Interpreting the Resurrection

The International Theological Commission provides the next hermeneutical tool for grounding a correct understanding of the resurrection by studying, understanding, believing, and trusting the Creed and the doctrines of the Fathers of the Church. In the Creeds, "there are dogmatic formulas of a very realistic kind referring to the body of the resurrection."[216] Thus it is important to emphasize that the resurrection will take place in this flesh which in we now live.[217] The Fathers purport that personal identity cannot exist without bodily identity. Therefore, such hermeneutics will correct many fundamental notions of discontinuity about life and life after death. These hermeneutical/interpretive tools, then, open the way to pastoral applicability for understanding and communicating to contemporary society to intentionally live eschatologically as a preamble to the final consummation in the beatific vision.

3.2. Pastoral Applicability for Better Contemporary Eschatological Living

After understanding these hermeneutical tools, it is necessary for us to see how pastors and evangelizers can apply these tools to contemporary lives to expand the human horizon beyond Marxism/utopianism, skepticism, and discontinuity theories presented in Chapter One continue to affect our living eschatologically. This task involves a kenosis from those who already understand and strive to live

---

[216] International Theological Commission, *Some Current Questions in Eschatology*, 64.

[217] Fides Damasi (NY: Oxford University Press, 2009), 72.

eschatologically to help those who either have never heard about life after death, or who know only the pleasures of this world (Mat. 13) which continues to choke them. The mission of the Church in gaining souls for the Kingdom is eternally urgent.

3.2.1. The Role of the Church in Instilling Eschatological Consciousness

Paul says, "for none of us lives for ourselves alone, and none of us dies for ourselves alone. If we live, we live for the Lord; and if we die, we die for the Lord. So, whether we live or die, we belong to the Lord" (Rom 14:7). This passage tells us that whether we are aware or not, we belong to the Lord. In beautiful fashion, Paul shows the Church as the principal agent and locus in bringing about eschatological consciousness, because Jesus, who came and died for us, left us a missionary mandate to work at saving souls for him, so that in both living and dying, we should always belong to the Lord.

The Church uniquely has been given the knowledge of the mysteries of salvation. Among those she tries to evangelize are people who have never heard the word of God, those who have heard and it has passed them without bearing fruit[218] and, most importantly for our purposes in this paper, those who have encountered incorrect eschatological theories like scientific materialism, Marxism, and millennialism, and they have had a deep impression made on them that has changed their worldview drastically. Therefore, instilling, and reinstalling eschatological consciousness is beautifully captured by *Evangelii Nuntiandi*:

---

[218] Paul VI, *Evangelii Nuntiandi*, n. 52.

> *Evangelization cannot but include the prophetic proclamation of a hereafter, man's profound and definitive calling, in both continuity and discontinuity with the present situation: beyond time and history, beyond the transient reality of this world, and beyond the things of this world, of which a hidden dimension will one day be revealed-beyond man himself, whose true destiny is not restricted to this temporal aspect but will be revealed in the future life.[219]*

The Church's role as *cura animarum* is more urgent in making everyone conscious because even though it is a given that we belong to the Lord, it is not a given that we shall all be saved; so, she needs to continually make this message clear and reach more people because the day of the Lord comes to all of us unannounced.[220] For instance, secularization has brought about a lack of consciousness about God and the life after. It's a norm in many parts of America that after confirmation, kids are only seen in Church when they come for their wedding ceremonies. They do not think of the end times. Attending church has become a formality to please parents.

Preaching about eschatological consciousness is more needed than ever. As *Evangelii Nuntiandi* (*EN*) writes, "evangelization cannot but include the prophetic proclamation of the hereafter."[221] Evangelizers need to feel comfortable talking about eschatological consciousness because it is true

---

[219] Paul VI, *Evangelii Nuntiandi* (Libreria Vaticana Editrice: Vatican, 1975) n.28.

[220] Scott Gleaves, "The Ethics of 2 Peter: The Impact of an Eschatological Consciousness," in Iineymatika (2014), 83-95.

[221] Paul VI, *Evangelii Nuntiandi*, n.28.

of every human being that we shall die. How can pastors go about this?

3.2.2. Pastors and Evangelizers as Immediate Respondents

Pastors need to reimagine ways of prophetically reaching out to those in the pews and beyond in a manner that does not scare them about the end times but encourages them to return to Church and prepare for Day of the Lord. The New Evangelization encourages new ardor, expression, and methods. "New in ardor" means that pastors give evangelization a style that will sound different to the hearers and make a deep impression on them. "In expression" can be synonymous to poetically expressing the Gospel in a manner that can be described as seductive and transformative to the listeners. And by "method," preachers need to change from archaic ways of expressing the Gospel, which is already far removed in time. Adequate exegesis and understanding of the text can only be the fruit of adequate contemplation and understanding of the surroundings.[222] David Hebert writes of a need for "radical eschatology," which involves going back to the roots: "an eschatology that is radical in this sense asks for the deepest reason and foundation of Christian hope, in which it is grounded on God's acting."[223] Radical eschatology is the way pastors and evangelizers act as first respondents to the declining consciousness in eschatology and the Gospel. Hebert makes it clear that to solve any problem, we need to get back to the roots. Therefore, when pastors and

---

[222] Boniface Hicks, New Evangelization: New in its ardor, methods and expression, https://www.fatherboniface.org/wordpresshome/new-evangelization/new-evangelization-new-in-its-ardor-methods-and-expression/ (accessed on the 17th of October 2021).

[223] David Hebert, *The Need for Teaching the Eschatological Gospel of Both Comings of Jesus Christ in the 21st Century* (2009), 3.

evangelizers in American parishes target Confirmation classes, it is important to ask them why it is that, after confirmation, the Church is no longer valuable for new members. It is necessary too to know what could be done differently for members to come back to church and love coming to church.

Targeting the hopes and aspirations of the newly confirmed is an excellent strategy. Therefore, it is necessary to know what they hope for and what they need, and then to inculcate those in catechesis with the ultimate hope, which is to be with God. This hope should not be a futuristic eschatology of Moltmann and Pannenberg, or a secular existentialist/preterist eschatology, but it should be hope that is built from living eschatologically towards the eternal kingdom. If pastors and evangelizers can show that their hopes and aspirations feed on the hope at the end of the world, this could attract more to remain true to the Church. For instance, in St Joseph's parish in Cockeysville, Maryland, there was always a struggle to have the confirmation kids enroll in a particular service/outreach or ministry in the parish. The pastor, Rick Hilgartner, explains that they have noticed that once they have something to do, they will always have a reason to come back.[224] They do not necessarily hate God, and they are not totally indifferent about the end times. Their problem is that they need to channel their energy and feel useful, and they feel there is still time since most of the people in the pews are old people. Therefore, a radical eschatology

---

[224] Msgr. Rick Hilgartner is a pastor of St Joseph Parish in Cockeysville, MD. The account presented here is based on my personal encounter with Msgr. Rick Hilgartner who is the pastor of St Joseph in Cockeysville where I interned for a year.

will help rekindle and foster eschatological consciousness in every target population.

Also, there is need for some form of eschatological preaching to be incorporated into the homilies of pastors. It is true that throughout the liturgical year, there are not many instances when such moments arise, but pastors need to make it a habit to preach eschatologically to remind people of the need to always be prepared. Advent, accordingly, is a very important season to preach about the end times because from the moment Christ came to redeem us, he won us for God. During Advent, we wait our redemption, which Christ came to fulfill.[225]

Truly, the coming of Jesus Christ was primarily to bring the Good News of salvation. The Good News opens history to the initiative of God and the human heart to the divine initiative so that humanity, history, and heaven can come together in fullness in Jesus Christ.[226] It is important to preach this Good News and open avenues for people to hear it and be saved, but this cannot be the end. But the Good News needs to be preached in ways that will not drive people away; we need to preach that there is an end, and we must merit it. Universally, Christ's coming and dying won salvation for us, but the individual redemption of each soul is worked for by everyone.[227] Thus, preachers need to continually make that awareness of an end time and the need to be prepared before

---

[225] Bud Stevens. This conversation took place on the 28th of May 2021 as he explained to me the importance of eschatological preaching and how vivid Advent can be a reason for that to be incorporated into the preaching of pastors.

[226] Darin W. Synder, *Good News: The Advent of Salvation in the Gospel of Luke* (MN: Liturgical Press, Collegeville, 2014), Chapter 1.

[227] Jay Wilson, *God's Plan of Salvation,* 30, unpublished.

it takes us away, like a thief, and Christ's self-giving on the cross is a very important way.

3.2.3. Kenosis of the Cross

In Phil. 2.4-13, Paul gives a wonderful text on the kenosis of Christ and prefaced this text with an ethical instruction calling on the Philippians and us to "look to the interests of others, not your own."[228] This is important to do because Jesus Christ, who "though he was in the form of God, did not regard equality with God as something to be grasped at but emptied himself (ekenōsen) taking the form of a slave" (Phil. 2). Jesus did not look upon himself, but continually thought of others. Other translations talk of "grasped at" (v.6) as something to be exploited. In the world, people constantly exploit others for their self-gain. People stop doing certain things just because they do not know what they will gain from it. However, Jesus' kenosis brings a new way of acting and living. He empties himself and takes human form not for his own sake, but for the common good of humanity.

This self-emptying of God, unlike what Moltmann says, cannot be "self-withdrawing." Moltmann says that God "withdrew himself into himself in order to make room for the world."[229] On the cross, Jesus freely and willingly emptied himself for the good of humanity. In living eschatologically, Christ's self-emptying (kenosis) must be the model we follow. For instance, in relation to theories of life after death like

---

[228] Thomas Jay Oord, *The Uncontrolling Love of God: An Open and Relational Account of Providence* (Illinois: InterVarsity Press, Downers Grove, 2015), 154.

[229] Jürgen Moltmann, "God's Kenosis in the Creation and Consummation of the World," in *The Work of Love: Creation as Kenosis, ed.* John C. Polkinghorne (MI: Grand Rapids, Eerdmans, 2001), 146.

millennialism, nihilism, existentialism, and so on, proponents of these theories, as I see it, need to do two things. First, they need to withdraw from teaching and propounding tepid and discontinuous theories that mislead the masses. This is important because these teachings are wrong and continue to mislead others from living eschatologically. Second, they need to understand the authentic teaching about life after death and begin to empty themselves in the *same* manner in which they have taught wrong doctrine. Therefore, contemporary man needs to learn from the kenosis of the cross so that, like Christ who died for humanity, we can die in little ways to help others live for God and prepare themselves for the life to come. This is important because we form our identity through kenosis and rivalry.[230]

3.3. Pastoral Care in the Sight of Death

Pastoral care in the coming of death is an important part of the ministry of the Church because it brings both the minister and the persons involved together, reflecting on eschatological issues. Paul Ballad says pastoral care consists of "helping acts, done by representative Christian persons, directed towards the healing, sustaining, guiding and reconciling of troubled persons whose troubles arise in the context of ultimate meanings and concerns."[231] Ballad makes

---

[231] It is worthy of note that according to Paul Ballad, pastoral care is much wider than just active in the sight of death. In his words, "it involves helping men and women to find their complete selves. It is an educative [and religious] process that has to take account of the brokenness, weakness and failings of human nature as well as its joys, hopes and creative potentials." This entails that it is wider than just being limited to death but for the purposes of this paper, it shall be limited to pastoral care in the sight of death. (Paul Ballad, *Pastoral Care* in "Christianity the Complete Guide," eds. John Bowden et al, (London: Continuum, 2020, 892-895.

it clear that it is done by "representative Christian persons."[232] This is important because it involves eschatological matters, so persons trained in these realities need to take charge of such an important ministry in the "context of ultimate meanings and concerns."[233] This section shall therefore examine the return of the unchurched at funerals, grieving ministries of Hope, and a reconsideration of Funeral Homilies.

3.3.1. The Return of the Unchurched at Funeral Masses

Funerals bring people together to console each other at the passing of a loved one. When we encounter death, people of different faith backgrounds and different states in life pray with the family. As difficult as funerals are for families and those present, it is an important moment for evangelization. In this way, it is important that parishes and funeral ministers are kind and patient with those who attend because they are not the regular crowd at Sunday or weekday liturgies. There may be unchurched people or nominal Christians who fell away for reasons we may never know. Thus, making churches welcoming and supportive at this time can bring many back. For instance, Msgr. Charles Pope says he has changed his approach at funerals and weddings because he encounters a lot of fallen away Christians. He calls their consciences to return to the Lord, praying for them to be at a right relation with God. As hard as this is, it is important to use this opportunity to talk to the congregation

---

[232] Paul Ballad, *Pastoral Care* in "Christianity the Complete Guide," 892-895.

[233] Paul Ballad, *Pastoral Care* in "Christianity the Complete Guide," 892-895.

since it is a great medium for evangelization.[234] In this way, the funeral becomes the place of evangelization; preaching is paramount to this endeavor.

3.2.2. A Reconsideration of Funeral Homilies

Funeral homilies should not be eulogies or a canonization of the dead person, because judgement about heaven and hell belongs only to God, who does not see as man sees. This does not negate mentioning the dead person, but it should not be a praise of the person, whom the preacher may not know well. As clergy, we celebrate funerals for people we do not know and have never met. Therefore, referring to some points about the person's life should be supported by how one received this information. Despite how consoling it may be to the family, it is out of place to claim there is now an angel in Heaven praying and interceding for us, just as it is out of place to say this soul is already in hell. The admonition "Do not judge" applies here with rigid impartiality such that preachers do not preach people into heaven or into hell. Eschatological realities are hidden from us, so we can only implore on God's mercy while exhorting those present to better their lives as they journey towards the end. This funeral homily preached by Jude T. Sango at the funeral of "George" gives important insights for funeral homilies:

> We are all gathered here today by the common
> human experience of tears. But there is
> something bigger than tears which brings us
> here together, it is something more sublime, it is
> something really honorable, it is something so

---

[234] Charles Pope, *Talking (Tough) Truth at Funerals*, http://blog.adw.org/2009/12/talking-truth-at-funerals/ (accessed on October 10 2021.

majestic, it is something with a supernatural orientation - I call that something Faith. So it is that while tears bring us together to share our sorrow of death, faith brings us together to share our hope of life after death. So it is that while tears bring us together to weep at the departure of our husband, father, uncle and friend George; faith brings us together to a new kind of being with our husband, father, uncle and friend George. So it is that while our tears bring us together to whisper how it is that yesterday a woman was married and today, we call her a widow, our faith brings us together to embrace a God who is the husband of the widows. While our tears bring us together to feel the pain of children who had a father yesterday and today, we call them orphans, faith brings us together to celebrate a God who fathers the fatherless. So it is that while tears gather us to cry over what we see as our common end, faith brings us together to celebrate our common transition to new life. It is so because even though we die in the body, we live in the spirit. And faith tells us that there is a part of us that does not die - the soul. The soul lives on because our faith tells us that death has no power to kill that which cannot die. Among us there is silence as if we are waiting to hear the voice of our husband, father, uncle and friend.

In our eyes there are tears. Our hearts are broken. Yet in our silence, God speaks to us: "there is a time for everything, and God's time is

101

the best." In our tears God consoles us, for "even tears cannot separate us from the love of God." In our brokenness and broken hearts, God whispers to us, "do not let your hearts be troubled, trust in God and trust in me." This is how the word of God consoles us and it does not do so because it is sweet to hear, it does so because it is true.

Death means different things to different people: to the pagans, death is the end, a certain annihilation- that is why we have this adage (said when we claim to be enjoying life) – after life comes death. For a Christian life does not end at death and so for the Christian, the adage will be after life comes death and after death comes life. So death is not the end for Christians but another beginning. So if we die because we were born, even more we live because we died.

The paradox of Christian life is that our death is in our life and our life is in our death. Death comes to us all: death is not moved by the innocence of the child. Death is not frightened by the muscles of a wrestler. Death is not seduced by the beauty of the young lady. Death is not even touched by the holiness of the priest. The worst about death is that there can be no representatives. It is something that each and all must face in his or her own respect and time. We try to make death beautiful, with nice coffins and beautiful parties and flowers but in our eyes, death remains that unfeeling reality, cruelly pulling asunder those joined in love, friendship and blood. We know that we all have to face death, but we still fear death. I had an experience as a very young priest, on Ash Wednesday 2018. Two boys came to me in Cameroon and said at the insistence of their dad, they needed to receive ashes to have dinner that evening. I asked them to go to Church and wait for me to come. When I came, I said I had to explain what ashes mean and why we take it. I told them that it means we shall die (you are dust and unto dust you shall return). They retorted that it is better they do not have dinner that night than to willingly accept that. We all fear death, but we shall still have to face it. Therefore, as we continue to pray for the repose of the soul of George, we pray that God will forgive him of all his sins and take him to his bosom to enjoy eternal peace.[235]

It is worth noting that in this homily, Fr. Jude constantly shows the place of God in our lives, stressing that we may feel we walk alone, but God is walking with us. He does not get into any praise of the dead person but shows that even though death is a universal phenomenon, we all fear to encounter it. He does not canonize the dead person as an angel but shows how we need to prepare for our own death so that we can enjoy eternal bliss with God. Given that death does not fear anyone, it is important to be adequately prepared for it than to be taken unawares.

---

[235] Jude T. Sango, Homily delivered at the occasion of the wake keep mass of George at Leesburg Virginia, October 2021 (Unpublished Homily).

3.3.3. Grieving Ministries of Hope

When we grieve, "we are not simply grieving the loss of one we have loved, we are also grieving the loss of the narrative by which we have lived our lives."[236] Thus, grief does not end with burial, but continues. As pastors, it is important for us to provide resources to people who are going through grief so that they can walk through their loss with the assurance of a faith community, pastoral staff, and people undergoing similar hardships. Therefore, it is important that parishes provide such ministries to instill hope in families following their loss. Grief should not aim so much at closure given that we carry in us the death of Jesus Christ, and every day brings us closer to our eschatological end; so, those grieving should be taught to "pray that all of our lost loves will be gathered into that great unending story fashioned by God's grace."[237]

Hope is important in Catholic grieving because life does not end at death. After death there is still life, so grieving ministries should be tailored to help bereaved families think about the hope in the life to come rather than look at the loss of their loved ones as the end of life. These ministries are important also as a way to correct those theories of hope that go against the belief in life after death. For instance, occasionally some of those grieving out of emptiness feel life is ended in death. Thus, through a reassurance of the

---

[236] Thomas G. Long, *The Good Funeral: Death, Grief, and the Community Care* (Westminster: John Knox Press, 2013), 224.

[237] Long, *The Good Funeral*, 225.

resurrection and eternal life for the dead, through our prayers, we can be assured of once again seeing our loved ones.

*if you are enjoying this book leave a review for the author on amazon **Thank you!***

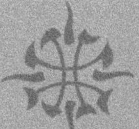

CONCLUSION

I n this work, I set out to examine an understanding of life after death as a prerequisite to interpreting and unlocking different lived expressions of life in society today. This brought us to the conclusion that the way one understands life after death greatly determines the way one lives in this world. The state of the problem today shows misunderstanding and rejection of an authentic understanding to living eschatologically. There is lack of biblical understanding of life after death, as people continually think that there is no biblical foundation for life after death. Others think that progress in the physical sciences is not compatible with living eschatologically, and the continual secularization in the world has given people less interest in living eschatologically.

In examining prominent theories about life after death, these theories show discontinuity in living a "realized and not yet" eschatology. Theories like existential eschatology, futuristic eschatology, reincarnation, millennialism, and so on are one-sided. In asserting that reincarnation is a possibility, the adherents of this theory teach that there is always time for renewal because after death we have another form of existence to purify ourselves if we died in a state of impurity. The effect of these theories is to live not in accordance with the kingdom of God but in accordance with our own whims and caprices despite the authentic way that Christians are called to live.

Chapter two brought forth a correct understanding of what the Church teaches about life after death. I examined the biblical understanding of life after death, immortality of the soul, the resurrection of Christ as a foundation for our own resurrection, purgatory, and heaven and hell as ways to debunk theories of limitation that prevent Christians from living eschatologically. The chapter culminated with the fact that even for an eschatological skeptic, it is better to wager for life after death as Blaise Pascal said so that if at death there is no life after death, one would not lose anything, rather than to die and cry like the rich man who solicited for water to quench his thirst in *Gehenna*.

Chapter three looked at the hermeneutical tools of interpreting today's lived expressions toward pastoral applicability in our today's world. These tools show that the acceptance of revealed truths, the basis of the resurrection, and a correct criterial for interpretation are important principles regarding life after death and how it translates in our lived experiences today. The loss of the sense of the sacred is directly proportional to the loss of interest in living eschatologically, as revelation counts for little or nothing to many who want to see and experience life. Therefore, evangelizers need to bring to the consciousness of their congregation the importance of being aware of the end times and striving to live accordingly. Among the avenues for such are incorporating eschatological concepts in their preaching and using funerals as a means to evangelize all present in authentic eschatological living and the need to work for salvation in fear and trembling. Despite the feelings and emotions at funerals, good doctrine should still triumph rather than statements that contradict what we teach and believe about eschatology.

This work, therefore, sought to interpret the contemporary style of living from an understanding of death. In this respect, the following conclusions can be drawn. Understanding the rationale behind an understanding of life after death makes it easy to see how an atheist or as Christians live their lives here on earth. The numerous secular belief systems in our society continually plague thousands of people in the way they live on this earth. A correct understanding of life after death needs to be taught and explained as even fervent Christians continue to struggle with this doctrine of the ultimate end. Finally, a return to metaphysical causality will bring back a sense of the sacred and reconstruct the finality of death from the limitations and discontinuities that prominent theories in the contemporary world expound to continue to trivialize authentic understanding and living in today's society. This is important because the end cause, eschatology, will always be in view as we all live for heaven knowing that eschatology is the first conceived but the last to be achieved based on how we live on earth. A good death is not wholly determined by what happens on the day we die but the consistent living out of our Christian calling throughout our lives is the real preparation for death. This paper is not exhaustive and has suggested further research considerations, like a deconstruction of present living in the light of the heaven and how present lived circumstances could be used and interpreted to draw people closer to God and overcoming a hermeneutical discontinuity in eschatology.

BIBLIOGRAPHY

Antonio, Orbe. *Anthropologia de San Ireneo.* Madrid: Valentino, 1969.

Augustine. *De Civitate Dei.* Tonholti: Brepols, 1955.

—. *The Confessions.* Trans. E.B Pusey, Portland, OR: The Floating Press, 2008.

Warfield, Benjamin. *Revelation and Inspiration.* New York: Oxford University Press, 1927.

Bühler, Pierre. eds. John Bowden, Anders Bergquist, Hugh Bowden, Norman A. Jjelm, Margaret Lydamore, "Hermeneutical Theology." *Christianity: The Complete Guide,* 2005.

Ballad, Paul. eds. John Bowden, Anders Bergquist, Hugh Bowden, Norman A. Jjelm, Margaret Lydamore "Pastoral Care." *Christianity: The Complete Guide.* London: Continuum, 2005.

Von Balthasar, Hans Urs. *The Mystery of Easter.* Edinburgh: T&T Clark, 1990.

Bauer, W. *Briechisch-deutsches Wörterbuch zu den schriften des Neuen Testaments und der   ubrigen urchristlichen Literatu.* Berlin, 1958.

Bond, Helen K. *The Historical Jesus: A Guide for the Perplexed.* London: T&T Clark, Edinburg   2020.

Bowden, John. eds. John Bowden, Anders Bergquist, Hugh Bowden, Norman A. Jjelm, Margaret

Lydamore "Life After Death." *Christianity: The Complete Guide*. London: Continuum, 2005.

Bruce, Steve. *Secularization: In Defense of an Unfashionable Theory.* Oxford: Oxford   University Press, 2011.

Campbell, Joseph Kiem, et al. *Freedom and Determinism.* Cambridge MA: Bradford Book,   2004.

Carmignac, Jean. *Les Dangers de l'eschatologie.* Paris: Letouzey et Ane, 1978.

Carole, Susan B. *Called to Communion: A Paradigm Shift in Holiness Theology.* OR: Wipf

and Stock Publishers, 2013.

Copleston, Frederick. *A History of Philosophy.* New York: Newman, 1975.

Cox, Harvey. *The Secular City.* London: Pelican Books, 1968.

Cumont, Franz. *Lux Perpetua.* Paris: Leuven, 1949.

Dollard, Jerome. "Eschatology, A Roman Catholic Perspective." *Review and Expositor*, vol. 79   no. 2 (MONTH?/QAURTER? 1964): 367-380.

Danielou, Jean. *Son Univers [de Origenes] est un monde de libertes, Origene.* Paris, 1948.

Darwin, Charles. *The Origin of Species by Means of Natural Selection, or the Preservation of Favoured Races in the Struggle for Life.* Chicago: Agate Publishing, 1952.

Date, Christopher M. "The Hermeneutics of Conditionalism: A Defense of the Interpretive   Method of Edward Fudge." *The Evangelical Quarterly* 74 (2018): 71-90.

Downing, F. G. *Has Christianity a Revelation?* London: SCM, 1964.

Dulles, Avery. *Revelation and Reason.* Westminster: P&P Publishing, 1964.

Eugenio, Dick O. *Communion with The Triune God: The Trinitarian Soteriology of T. F.   Torrance.* Cambridge: James Clarke & Co, 2014.

Congregation of the Doctrine of the Faith. *Libertatis Nuntius.* Vatican City: Editrice   Vaticana, 1984.

Congregation of the Doctrine of the Faith, *Responses to Some Questions Regarding Certain*

Aspects of the Doctrine on the Church. Washington D.C.: USCCB, 2012.

—. *Recentiores Episcoporum Synodi.* Vatican City: Vaticana, 1979.

Feuerbach, Ludwig. *Die Unsterbllichkeitsfrage vom Standpunkt der Anthropologie.* Germany, 1970.

Fieser, Samuel E. Stumpf and James. *Philosophy: History and Problems.* New York: McGraw Hill Publishing, 2007.

Hampton, Jim and Amy Brothers. *Sacred Time Living in the Presence of God.* Kansas City: Barefoot Ministries, 2009.

Synod of Bishops. *Relatio Finalis.* Vaticana: E. Civitate, 1985.

Fischer, Johann. "Das Buch Der Weischeit." *Exhter Bibel*, 1959: 723.

—. *Das Buch Isaias.* Bonn: I. Teil, 1937.

Fletcher, Jeannine Hill. *Eschatology in Systematic Theology: Roman Catholic Perspective.*   Minneapolis: Fortress Press, 2011.

Gilson, Étienne. *The Christian Philosophy of Saint Augustine.* Rhode Island: Providenc Cluny, 2020.

Gleaves, Scott. "The Ethics of 2 Peter: The Impact of an Eschatological Consciousness." *Iineymatika* Vol? No? (2014): 83-95.

Gunton, Collin E. *Intellect and Action: Christian Theology and the Life of Faith.* Edinburgh: T&T Clark, 2019.

Hardon, John A. *The Doctrine of Purgatory.* San Francisco: Ignatius Press, 2001.

Healy, Nicholas J. *The Eschatology of Hans Urs von Balthasar.* Oxford: Oxford University   Press, 2005.

Heidegger, Martin. *Being and Time.* London: SCM, 1962.

Henry, Carl F. H. "The Priority of Divine Revelation: A Review." *The Journal of the   Evangelical Theological Society* 27:1 (1984): 77-92.

Hick, John. *Death and Eternal Life.* New York: Harper, 1976.

Hicks, Boniface. "New Evangelization: New in its Ardor, Methods, and Expressions." *Father   Boniface Hicks, O.S.B.* (blog), July 28, 2017.
        https://www.fatherboniface.org/wordpresshome/new-evangelization/new-evangelization-   new-in-its-ardor-methods-and-expression/ (accessed October 17, 2021).

John Paul II. General Audience. July 28, 1999. www.vatican.va/holy_father/john_ii/audiences/1999/documents/hf_jp-   ii_aud_28071999_en.html (accessed October 9, 2021)

Hobbes, Thomas. *On the Citizen.* Edited by Richard Tuck and Michael Silverthorne. MA: Cambridge: Cambridge University Press, 1998.

Ingerson, Scofield C. *New Scofield Reference Bible.* New York: Oxford University Press, 1983.

Jaspers, Karl. *Philosophical Faith and Revelation.* New York: Harper, 1967.

Jerome. *Fides Damasi.* Oxford: Oxford University Press, 2009.

Judisch, Neal. "Theological Determinsim and the Problem of Evil." *Religious Studies* 44 (2008):   165-184.

K.G., Bretschneider. "Versuch einer systematischen Entwickelung aller." *der Dogmatik   vorkommenden Begriff*, (1805): 476.

Kathleen, Fischer R. *El pensamiento de Etienne Gilson.* Pamplona, Spain: 1980.

Kehl, Medard. *Eschatology.* Wurzburg: Echter, 1986.

Kreeft, Peter J. *Catholic Christianity: A Complete Catechism of Catholic Beliefs Based on the Catechism of the Catholic Church.* San Francisco: Ignatius Press, 2001.

Kuupuo, Sev. "He Descended into Hell." *St. Thomas Aquinas Parish* (news). August 13, 2019. https://paloaltocatholic.net/news/he-descended-into-hell (accessed September 23, 2021).

Long, Thomas G. *The Good Funeral: Death, Grief, and the Community Care.* Westminster: John Knox Press, 2013.

Ludwig, Feuerbach. *The Essence of Christianity.* New York: Harper Torchbooks, 1957.

Marcel, Gabriel. *Homo Viator: Introduction to the Metaphysics of Hope.* South Bend, IN: St. Augustine's Press, 2010.

Marx, Karl. *Thesis on Feuerbach.* New York: Schocken Books, 1964.

May, John L. *Order of Christian Funerals with Cremation Rite.* Totowa, NJ: Catholic Book Publishing Company, 2019.

Mark Jordan, Editor. *The Church's Confession of Faith: A Catholic Catechism for Adults.* San Francisco: Ignatius Press, 1987.

Moltmann, Jürgen. *God's Kenosis in the Creation and Consummation of the World.* Grand Rapids, MI: Eerdmans Publishing Company, 2001.

—. *Theology of Hope.* San Francisco: Harper, 1965.

Nietzsche, Freidrick. *Thus Spake Zarathustra .* New York: Macmillan, 1924.

Oord, Thomas Jay. *The Uncontrolling Love of God: An Open and Relational Account of Providence.* Downers Grove, IL: InterVarsity Press, 2015.

Machey, J.P. *Problems in Religious Faith.* Dublin: Helicon, 1972.

Pascal, Blaise. *Le Pensee.* New York: Collier & Son, 1910.

Petrakis, Vicki. "The Plasma as Salvation History in St Irenaeus of Lyons." *Phronema* 34 (2019): 103-123.

Phan, Peter C. "Current Theology Contemporary Context and Issues in Eschatology." *Theological Studies* 55 (1994): 507-536.

Plato. *The Republic.* Cambridge: Harvard University Press, 1953.

Pope, Charles. "Talking (Tough) Truth at Funerals." *Community in Mission* (blog). December 15, 2009. http://blog.adw.org/2009/12/talking-truth-at-funerals/ (accessed October 10, 2021).

Porphyry. *De Plotini vita 1: Plotin Schriften.* Volume 5. Edited by R. Harder.. Hamburg: Hamburg Press, 1958.

Prat, Fernan. *The Theology of St Paul.* Westmister: Newman Books, 1953.

Ratzinger, Joseph. *Introduction to Christianity.* San Francisco: Ignatius Press, 2004.

—. *Eschatology: Death and Eternal Life.* Washington D.C: The Catholic University of America, 1988.

—. *God is Near Us: The Eucharist, The Heart of Life.* San Francisco: Ignatius Press, 2003

—. *The Catechism of the Catholic Church.* Vatican: Libreria Editrice Vaticana, 2018.

Reith, Herman. *The Metaphysics of St. Thomas Aquinas.* Milwaukee: The Bruce Publishing Company, 1958.

Jude Sango Homily Delivered on the Occasion of the Wake Keep Mass of George at the Funeral

Home in Leeburg, September 2021, unpublished.

Sartre, Jean-Paul. *Being and Nothingness: An Essay on Phenomenological Ontology.* New York: Philosophical Library Press, 1956.

Scheffczyk, L. *Der Reinkarnatinsgedanke in der altchristlichen Literatur.* Manchen, 1985.

Schwarz, Hans. *Eschatology.* Grand Rapids, MI: William B. Eerdmans, 2000.

Sheen, Fulton J. *Life of Christ.* New York: McGraw-Hill Book Company, 1958.

Sharkey, Michael and Thomas Weinandy, Editors. "Some Current Questions in Eschatology." *International Theological Commission*, 1992: 55-93.

de la Soujeole, Benoît."Vocabulaire et notions a Vatican II et dans le magistere posterieur."   *Revue Thomiste* 110, (2010): 245-273.

__. *Introduction to the Mystery of the Church.* Washington D.C.: The Catholic University of   America Press, 2014.

Soyinka, Wole. *The Trials of Brother Jero.* Lagos: Dramatists Play Service, Inc., 1998.

Sullivan, Francis A. *The Church We Believe In.* New York: Paulist Press, 1988.

Synder, Darin W. *Good News: The Advent the Salvation in the Gospel of Luke.* Collegeville, MN: Liturgical Press, 2014.

Arnold, Bill T. "Old Testament Eschatology and the Rise of Apocalypticism in Historical   Eschatology," in *The Oxford Handbook of Eschatology*, ed., Jerry L. Walls, NY, Oxford University Press, 2008), 23-39.

Tournay, Robert. *La Sainte Bible.* Paris: Desclee, 1956.

Tuckett, Christopher. *2 Thessalonians and Pauline Eschatology.* Petters: Leuven, 2013.

Norman P. Tanner, ed., *Ecumenical Council of Florence.*

https://www.ewtn.com/catholicism/library/ecumenical-council-of-florence-1438-1445-1461 (accessed October 5, 2021).

Paul VI,. *Ad Gentes Divinitus.* Minneapolis: Liturgical Press, 1996.

—. *Dei Verbum.* Vatican City: Vatican Press, 1965.

—. *Dei Verbum.* Minneapolis: Liturgical Press, 1999.

—. *Evangelii Nuntiandi.* Vatican: Libreria Vaticana Editrice, 1975.

—. *Lumen Gentium.* Minneapolis: Liturgical Press, 1996.

—. *Professio Fidei.* Vatican: Libreria Editrice Vaticana, 1998.

—. *Unitatis Redintegration.* Minneapolis: Liturgical Press, 1999.

Vinzent, Markus. *Christ's Resurrection in Early Christianity and the Making of the New Testament.* Burlinton, VT: Ashgate Publishing Company, 2011.

Walvoord, John F. *The Rapture Question.* Grand Rapids, MI: Dunham, 1964.

Webster, John. *Word and Church: Essays in Christian Dogmatics.* Edinburgh: T&T Clark, 2001.

White, Bob. *Jesus, The Complete Guide.* London, 2020.

Williamson, Peter S. *Revelation: Catholic Commentary on Scripture.* Michigan: Baker Academics, 2015.

Pannenberg, Wolfhart. *Systematic Theology.* Grand Rapids, MI: Eerdmans Publishing, 1991.

Wood, Shevington A. "The Eschatology of Irenaeus." *The Evangelical Quarterly* 41.1 (1969): 30-41.

---

if you are enjoying this book leave a review for the author on amazon
Thank you!